Miriam's
Cookbook

Other Books by Carrie Bender

A Fruitful Vine
A Winding Path
A Joyous Heart
A Treasured Friendship
A Golden Sunbeam

WHISPERING BROOK SERIES

Whispering Brook Farm
Summerville Days
Chestnut Ridge Acres

Carrie Bender

Miriam's Cookbook

Compiled and Edited by Mary Clemens Meyer

Herald
Press

Herald Press
Scottdale, Pennsylvania
Waterloo, Ontario

Library of Congress Cataloging-in-Publication Data
Bender, Carrie, date
    Miriam's cookbook / Carrie Bender; compiled and edited by Mary
Clemens Meyer.
       p. cm.
    Includes bibliographical references and index.
    ISBN 0-8361-9086-6 (alk. paper)
    1. Cookery, Amish. I. Meyer, Mary Clemens, 1954-   . II. Title.
TX715.B466   1998
641.5'66—dc21   97-51939

The paper in this publication is recycled and meets the minimum re-
quirements of American National Standard for Information Sciences—
Permanence of Paper for Printed Library Materials, ANSI Z39.48-1984.

Recipe sources and permissions are listed on pages 127-128. The
excerpts from Miriam's Journal and the Whispering Brook Series are used
by permission of Herald Press, all rights reserved, with slight adaptations
for copyfitting.

MIRIAM'S COOKBOOK

Contents

Abbreviations

approx.	approximately
c.	cup (250 milliliters), cups
lb.	pound (500 grams), pounds
med.	medium
opt.	optional
oz.	ounce, ounces
pkg.	package, packages
pt.	pint (½ liter), pints
qt.	quart (1 liter), quarts
T.	tablespoon (30 milliliters), tablespoons
t.	teaspoon (10 milliliters), teaspoons

Preface

Welcome to Miriam's kitchen, glowing with the warmth of Amish family life. Here each season brings its bounty from garden and fields—spring strawberries and peas; summer sweet corn, beans, and tomatoes; autumn pumpkins and crisp, tangy apples. In the long evenings of the frosty cold winter, there is time to sit by the woodstove with a bowl of popcorn.

—Mary Clemens Meyer

A Cozy Kitchen

October 7

Fire in the range feels good this morning. I'm drying a pan of Yellow Delicious apples on top of the stove, and it's filling the kitchen with a delightful, sweet, tangy aroma.

The merits of the old kitchen range are varied and many, and I wonder why some folks prefer gas or oil heat. Besides cooking and baking with it and drying Schnitz (sliced apples) on top, the range heats water in the reservoir and teakettle for a variety of purposes—doing dishes, washing laundry, and taking baths.

Clothing can be dried around its glowing warmth (who needs an electric clothes dryer?) and sadirons heated for ironing clothes.

What feels better on a cold winter evening when you come in, half frozen from doing chores, than to stick your feet into the bake oven until they're toasty warm? The pipe shelf is great for drying mittens, and the warming closet keeps crackers and pretzels fresh.

The children like to make potato chips by laying thin-sliced potatoes on top of the stove until they're golden brown on each side, then sprinkling them with salt.

Last but not least is its usefulness in making toast. We either place bread slices on back of the stove for a while, or spear the bread with a fork, lift the lid, and toast it over the flame.

Chopping wood and carrying coal and ashes is well worth all these benefits. What would a farmhouse be without the good old cookstove? When the electric goes off during a storm, we're snug and warm, while our *englisch* neighbors are without heat.

(*A Joyous Heart*, 155-156)

Breakfast Specials

1

Breakfast Specials

August 30

Yesterday I woke to the familiar sound of the banty rooster crowing his welcome to the new day. I was thinking, How nice to wake up in my own bed.

I was singing as I sliced the mush into the pan to fry it and put on a kettle of water for the oatmeal with raisins. When I ran to the milk house for a pitcher of milk, a carriage was coming in the lane, and it was Grandpa Dave.

"Good morning!" I called cheerily. "You're up bright and early."

(A Joyous Heart, 152)

Fried Cornmeal Mush

1 c. cornmeal	1 c. milk
1 t. salt	3 c. water

Bring water to a boil. Make a paste with cornmeal, salt, and milk. Add to boiling water, stirring until it returns to boiling. Cook for 15 to 20 minutes, stirring occasionally, then pour into deep baking dish. Let cool, then slice ¼ inch thick and fry on griddle or in skillet until golden brown on both sides.

Cleaning hint: To clean mush kettle, put 1 or 2 cups water into kettle. Add 1 teaspoon soda. Cover kettle and put on heat till water boils. Set kettle aside, but keep covered until dishwashing time.

Oatmeal with Raisins

1 c. rolled oats	Raisins
2 c. water	Dash of cinnamon
1/2 t. salt	

Bring water to a boil and add oats. Reduce heat and cook for 10 minutes. Add raisins and cinnamon, and continue cooking for 5 minutes. Serve with milk and honey, brown sugar, or cinnamon sugar.

September 14

When I was setting the table for breakfast, Martha asked, "Do you mind if I make breakfast this morning? I'd like to try one of my favorite recipes, a breakfast casserole."

I told her she surely could. Martha busily flitted around the kitchen, humming a merry little tune as she worked. She took out a casserole dish, and I'm not sure what all she put in besides lots of eggs, bread, cream, salt, and pepper.

This she put into the oven to bake. She was amazed at having to strike a match to light the gas oven (the pilot light conked out); she was used to an electric oven.

Martha put milk into a saucepan, brought it to a boil, added rolled oats, raisins, and English walnuts. It was a good breakfast, interesting and different from our usual fried eggs, mush, potatoes, and grapenuts or granola.

(A Golden Sunbeam, 25-26)

Oven Egg Casserole

5 eggs	2-3 c. grated cheese
1 t. salt	21/2 c. hot milk
dash pepper	1 qt. cubed bread

Beat eggs until lemon-colored. Add salt, pepper, and cheese, and mix well. Add hot milk and bread, and pour into greased baking pan. Bake 30 minutes or until set. Top with chopped parsley just before serving.

Miriam's Favorite Granola

10 c. oatmeal
2 c. wheat germ
1 to 2 c. brown sugar
1/2 c. vegetable oil
1/2 c. honey

1/3 to 1/2 c. peanut butter
2 t. vanilla
1 t. salt
2 c. raisins

Mix dry ingredients. Heat oil and honey until lukewarm, then stir in peanut butter and mix with dry ingredients. Pour mixture into shallow pans. Toast at 275° for 30 to 40 minutes or until golden brown, stirring occasionally. Add raisins after granola is toasted.

Variations: Omit peanut butter, and add 2 cups coconut and 1 small package of almonds before toasting; add nuts, wheat germ, or coconut *after* granola has been toasted; add whole wheat flour, sesame seeds, sunflower seeds, dates, or 1 to 2 teaspoons of cinnamon.

Miriam's Grapenuts

5 c. flour
2 c. sugar
3 t. salt
3 c. buttermilk

6 c. whole wheat flour
21/2 c. cane molasses
3 t. soda

Combine ingredients to make dough that is thick and hard to stir. Spread in shallow pan, and bake at 250° for 11/2 to 2 hours. Crumble by one of these methods: 1. While still warm, break into chunks and grate on slaw cutter; or whirl briefly in blender, about a cupful at a time; 2. Allow to cool thoroughly, then put through food grinder, coarse plate. Store in plastic bag or airtight container.

Nancy hurried with her chores. She wanted to surprise Mary and Jacob by making waffles for breakfast as a special treat. Nancy knew Mary had a waffle iron, for she had seen it in the cellarway.

In the kitchen, Mary sat on a rocker, watching Nancy mixing the batter.

"Oh, Nancy," she exclaimed, "words cannot express how *dankbaar* (thankful) I am that you're here and are such a good helper!"

Nancy put a clean white tablecloth on the table, and in the center she placed a bouquet of freshly cut gladioli. It made the table look so pretty. Then she hurried to finish making the waffles.

Beginner's luck was with Nancy. The waffles turned out crisp and light, delicious and golden-browned to perfection.

"*Wunderbaar gute* (wonderfully good)," Jacob pronounced them at the breakfast table, as he poured maple syrup over them. "Lucky the man that gets you for a cook, Nancy. Already you're almost as good a cook as Mary is."

(*Summerville Days*, 80-81)

Waffles

2 c. flour	6 T. melted butter
1 t. salt	2 eggs, separated
4 t. baking powder	1 1/2 c. milk
1 T. sugar	

Mix dry ingredients in bowl. Beat egg yolks, and add milk; combine with flour mixture. Add melted butter. Fold in stiffly beaten egg whites, and bake in hot waffle iron. Makes 6 waffles.

Easy Pancakes

2 c. self-rising flour	2 T. sugar
1/2 c. buttermilk	1 T. melted shortening
2 eggs	Milk

Mix ingredients, adding enough milk to make a nice batter. Fry pancakes on lightly greased griddle.

Pancake Syrup

1 1/4 c. brown sugar
3/4 c. white sugar
1/3 c. molasses OR corn syrup

1 c. water
1 t. vanilla OR maple
flavoring (opt.)

Bring sugar, molasses, and water to a boil, stirring constantly. Simmer on low heat for 5 minutes. Remove from heat and add vanilla.

Oatmeal Pancakes

2 c. all-purpose flour
2 c. whole wheat flour
2 c. quick oats
1 T. each of baking
powder, soda, salt

3 eggs, separated
1/2 c. cooking oil
1 1/2 quarts milk (approx.),
warmed to lukewarm

Mix dry ingredients thoroughly. Stir in egg yolks, oil, and lukewarm milk. Fold in beaten egg whites. Pour batter onto preheated, ungreased griddle, using about ¼ cup for each pancake. Turn once.

Apple Pancakes

2 c. flour
2 T. sugar
4 t. baking powder
1 t. salt

2 c. milk
2 eggs, separated
2 T. melted butter
1 c. peeled, grated apple

Mix flour, sugar, baking powder, and salt in mixing bowl. In small bowl, combine milk, well-beaten egg yolks, and butter; mix well. Add to flour mixture, and beat until smooth. Stir in grated apple; fold in beaten egg whites. Grease hot griddle for first pancakes only. Use 1/2 cup for each pancake; cook until puffy and bubbly. Turn and brown other side.

Miriam's Apple Bake

Slice 4 apples into baking dish. Sprinkle with cinnamon and sugar to taste. Melt 1 tablespoon butter and drizzle over apples. Make batter with 1 cup flour, 1/4 cup milk, and 1 teaspoon baking powder. Pour over apples, and bake at 350° for 25 minutes.

Breads

2

Breads

July 25

Oh, for a breath of fresh air. I am sitting here fanning myself. I just took four crusty golden loaves of bread out of the oven, and now a delicious aroma fills the kitchen.

(A Fruitful Vine, 60)

White Bread

1 pkg. dry yeast	2 t. salt
1/2 c. warm water	2 T. cooking oil
13/4 c. scalded milk	5 to 6 c. flour
2 T. sugar	

Dissolve yeast in warm water. Combine milk, sugar, salt, and oil; cool to lukewarm. Stir in yeast, mixing well. Add flour gradually; knead. Cover and let rise till doubled in bulk. Punch dough down; let rise again. Shape into 2 loaves and place in greased loaf pans. Let rise till doubled in bulk. Bake for 25 to 30 minutes at 350°.

Honey Oatmeal Bread

2 pkg. dry yeast
1 c. warm water
21/2 c. boiling water
2 c. quick oatmeal
1 c. honey OR part
   corn syrup

3/4 c. cooking oil
4 beaten eggs
2 T. salt
2 c. or more whole wheat flour
White unbleached flour

Dissolve yeast in cup of warm water. Pour boiling water over oatmeal and set aside to cool until lukewarm. Mix in rest of ingredients, except yeast and flour, and beat mixture well. Add yeast, and work in enough white flour to make nice, spongy dough that is not sticky. Grease top of dough, then let it rise. Knead it and let rise again. Divide into 3 loaves, and bake at 400° for 10 minutes, then at 350° for 25 to 30 minutes. A delicious, nourishing bread.

Potato Bread

1 medium-sized potato
1 qt. water
2 T. butter
3 t. salt

2 pkg. dry yeast
1 t. sugar
1 c. warm water
11 to 12 c. all-purpose flour

Cook diced, peeled potato in quart of water till tender. Drain potato, reserving the water, and mash until no lumps remain. Add mashed potato to reserved water, and stir in butter and salt. Let mixture cool until lukewarm. Dissolve yeast and sugar in 1 cup warm water, and let stand for 5 to 10 minutes. Gradually add 6 cups of flour to potato water, beating until smooth. Mix in yeast-sugar mixture, and beat thoroughly. Cover and let dough rise in warm place for about 2 hours. Then work in enough additional flour to make soft dough. Knead dough until smooth and satiny. Put in greased bowl, greasing top of dough. Cover and let rise till double in size, about 11/2 hours. Punch down dough, and divide into 3 loaves. Cover and let rise till double, about 30 to 40 minutes. Bake at 375° for 40 minutes.

It's time to take my whole wheat bread out of the oven, judging by the wonderful aroma in the kitchen, and I hear the pitter-patter of little feet coming down the stairs. My sweet, pink-cheeked, tousle-headed dears are waking up, and I'm glad to see them. I think we'll make some red valentine hearts together, with lace out around and a verse in the middle, to send to Matthew, Rosabeth, and Mary. Valentine's Day is for celebrating love! "My heart rejoices in the Lord. I rejoice in your salvation."

(A Joyous Heart, 14-15)

Best Whole Wheat Bread

2 c. milk	3 T. yeast
1/3 c., plus 2 T. shortening	1 c. very warm
1/3 c. sugar	water
1 T. salt	1 c. cold water
2 c. whole wheat flour	White unbleached flour

Scald milk, then add shortening, sugar, and salt, stirring till dissolved. Add whole wheat flour and beat rapidly with spoon. Dissolve yeast in warm water, then add with cold water to the flour mixture. Mix well, then add enough white flour to make nice, soft dough. Knead for 10 minutes. Let rise until double in size, then punch down and turn over in greased bowl. Let rise again until double, then shape dough into 3 loaves, "spanking" them quite hard to remove all air bubbles. Cover for 15 minutes, letting dough rise until double, then bake at 350° for 50 to 60 minutes.

One book says a kitchen should be a place of reverence, where the fragrance of newly baked bread mingles with contentment and peace so beautiful and serene that all who dwell there are filled with joy and happiness.

Well! How can I keep the kitchen a place of peace and reverence? It's the only well-heated room in the house unless we have company. So the kitchen is the center of activity and hubbub. When the weather is bad, the mats are full of rows of boots, and there are wet mittens on the stovepipe shelf.

When it's really cold outside, everyone crowds around the stove. When they're hungry, the center of attraction is the table or the gas refrigerator.

(A Golden Sunbeam, 64)

Pull Buns ("Pluckets")

1/3 c. sugar	1 yeast cake OR 1 pkg. dry yeast
1/3 c. melted butter	1/4 c. lukewarm water
1/2 t. salt	3 eggs, well-beaten
1 c. scalded milk	33/4 c. all-purpose flour (approx.)

Add sugar, butter, and salt to scalded milk. When lukewarm, add yeast (which has been dissolved in 1/4 cup lukewarm water), eggs, and just enough flour to make stiff batter. Cover and let rise until double in bulk, then knead and let rise again. Roll dough into small balls, about the size of walnuts, and dip in melted butter. Then roll each ball in mixture of the following:

3/4 c. sugar
1/2 c. chopped nuts
3 t. cinnamon

Pile balls loosely in ungreased tube pan, and let rise for 30 minutes. (Do not use pan with removable bottom.) Bake buns until brown, about 40 minutes, beginning at 400° for 10 minutes, then at 350°. Turn pan upside down and remove buns immediately, serving while warm. Buns will be stuck together, and each person plucks his own serving.

Raisin Cinnamon Rolls

1/2 c. milk	1/2 c. lukewarm water
11/2 t. salt	2 t. sugar
1/2 c. sugar	2 eggs, beaten
1/4 c. shortening	4 c. all-purpose flour

Scald milk, then add salt, sugar and shortening. Cool to lukewarm. Sprinkle yeast over ½ cup lukewarm water, with 2 teaspoons of sugar added. Let mixture stand for 10 to 15 minutes before stirring and adding to milk. Add beaten eggs, then work in about 4 cups flour. Cover and let rise until double in bulk. Divide dough in 2 parts and roll each half into 9-x-12-inch rectangle. Brush each half with melted butter and sprinkle with the following mixture:

1 c. brown sugar
2 T. cinnamon
2/3 c. raisins

Roll up rectangles as for jelly rolls. Cut into 1-inch slices and place on greased pans. Cover and let rise until double, then bake at 350° for about 35 minutes. Frost rolls while warm with the following icing:

1 c. powdered sugar
1/4 t. vanilla
Enough milk to make stiff icing

December 22

We're having Christmas dinner at our house this year, and Martha is wholeheartedly involved in preparing for it. She even skipped going to the school program yesterday. When I came home, the table was piled high with crisp, golden-brown doughnuts. She enlisted the girls' aid for dipping them into powdered sugar.

(*A Golden Sunbeam*, 159)

Yeast Doughnuts

6 c. all-purpose flour (or more)	1 c. scalded milk
1 c. lukewarm water	2 t. salt
2 yeast cakes OR 2 pkg.	3 T. sugar
dry yeast	1/2 c. shortening
1 T. sugar	3 eggs, beaten

Pour water over yeast, adding tablespoon of sugar. Stir and let stand. Meanwhile, pour scalded milk into bowl and add salt, 3 tablespoons of sugar, and shortening. When lukewarm, add water-yeast mixture and 3 cups of flour. Beat mixture until smooth, then add eggs and rest of flour. Let dough rise in warm place until double in size. Roll out, cut out doughnuts, and let them rise. Fry doughnuts in hot grease. Makes about 75 doughnuts.

Delicious Pumpkin Bread

1 2/3 c. all-purpose flour	1 1/3 c. sugar
1/4 t. baking powder	1/2 t. vanilla
1 t. soda	2 eggs
3/4 t. salt	1 c. mashed pumpkin
1/2 t. cinnamon	1/3 c. water
1/2 t. nutmeg	1/2 c. chopped walnuts
1/3 c. shortening	OR pecans

Grease 9-x-5-x-3-inch loaf pan. Mix flour, baking powder, soda, salt, and spices. Cream shortening, sugar, and vanilla; add eggs, one at a time, and beat thoroughly after each addition. Stir in pumpkin. Then add dry ingredients alternately with water, beating just until mixture is smooth. Be careful not to overbeat. Fold in nuts. Turn batter into pan and bake at 350° for 45 to 55 minutes. Turn bread out onto wire rack and allow to cool before storing in tight container.

Cornmeal Muffins

1 c. cornmeal
1 c. all-purpose flour
1/4 c. sugar
1 t. salt
4 t. baking powder

1 c. milk
2 eggs, beaten
4 T. melted butter OR
    shortening

Mix dry ingredients, then add milk, eggs, and melted shortening. Stir mixture quickly until dry ingredients are just moistened. Bake batter in greased muffin tins for about 20 minutes, at 400°.

Biscuits Supreme

2 c. all-purpose flour
1/2 t. salt
2 t. sugar
4 t. baking powder

1/2 t. cream of tartar
1/2 c. shortening
2/3 c. milk

Mix dry ingredients, then cut in shortening until mixture resembles coarse crumbs. Add milk all at once, and stir just until dough follows fork around the bowl. Roll out dough to 1/2-inch thickness. Cut with biscuit cutter and place biscuits on ungreased cookie sheet. Bake in hot oven (450°) for 10 to 12 minutes.

Main Dishes

3

Main Dishes

August 7

After the chores were finished, two carriages drove in the lane. What a surprise! Priscilla, Henry, and Miriam Joy breezed into the kitchen, carrying pizzas ready to bake, and Barbianne and Rudy brought a freezer full of hand-cranked, homemade ice cream.

We were all so glad to see them. Soon the kitchen was filled with the wonderful aroma of homemade pizzas baking. I felt hungrier than I ever was before in my life, and my willpower was fast disappearing.

At first I fought temptation, but by the time Priscilla took the pizza out of the oven, I had made my decision. So much for Gloria's old fad diet. It was entirely unbalanced anyway. No meat, no milk, no variety. Why did I ever let her brainwash me like that?

The pizza was scrumptious! I enjoyed every bite of it.

(*A Treasured Friendship*, 33)

Homemade Pizza

1 pkg. yeast	1/4 c. salad oil
1 c. warm water	3 c. flour
1 t. sugar	1 1/2 t. salt

Dissolve yeast in warm water, add sugar, salt, and oil, and mix well. Add half of flour and beat until there are no lumps. Gradually add remaining flour. Knead dough for 5 minutes. Take half of dough and roll out into 12-inch circle. Place on greased cookie sheet, leaving edges a little thicker than middle. Repeat procedure with other half of dough, and put on second cookie sheet. Let dough rise for 20 to 30 minutes. Brush top with salad oil.

1 lb. ground beef, cooked	1 t. oregano
3/4 c. chopped onions	2 c. tomato sauce
1/2 c. chopped green peppers	1/2 to 1 pound cheese, shredded

To make topping, cook ground beef, onions, and pepper together. Add rest of ingredients and continue cooking. Spread mixture over crust, top with cheese, and bake at 400° for 20 minutes or until done.

December 3

Hog butchering time again. Yesterday Nate sharpened all the knives, and we scrubbed the big iron kettle above the furnace, washed and scalded the sausage grinder, and fastened it to the old sawhorse. . . . The children like to sit astraddle the sawhorse to turn the grinder. Yes, softhearted Nate lets them stay home from school to help and to watch, much to their delight.

There's always much jovial bantering and visiting going on as we grind and slice and salt the meat, and strip the fat for lard. The big hams and shoulders will be hung from the crossbeams in the smokehouse until they are cured and just the right flavor.

Visions of tender home-cured baked ham, juicy sausages, and crisp bacon dance in our heads as we work.

(*A Golden Sunbeam*, 109-110)

Ham Loaf

2 lb. smoked ham (ground)	1 1/2 c. bread crumbs
2 lb. fresh pork (ground)	1 t. salt
2 eggs	1 t. pepper
1 1/2 c. milk	

Mix all ingredients together, and form mixture into ball. Mix glaze ingredients, pour over top, and bake at 325° for 2 hours.

Glaze:

1 1/2 c. brown sugar	1/2 c. water
1 t. dry mustard	1/2 c. vinegar

Schnitz un Gnepp

1 qt. dried apples (*Schnitz*)	1/4 t. pepper
3 lb. ham	4 t. baking powder
2 T. brown sugar	1 egg, well-beaten
2 c. flour	Milk
1 t. salt	3 T. melted butter

Wash dried apples, then cover with water to soak overnight. Cover ham with boiling water and boil for 3 hours. Add apples and water in which they were soaked and boil for 1 hour longer. Add sugar.

Make dumplings (*Gnepp*) by mixing the flour, salt, pepper, and baking powder. Stir in beaten egg, milk (enough to make fairly moist, stiff batter), and butter. Drop batter by tablespoons into hot ham and apples. Cover and cook for 15 minutes. Serve hot as a one-dish meal.

What a blessing it was to step into Rosemary's cheery, homey kitchen. It was like a bit of heaven to me, to be welcomed so warmly, and ushered in like that, after being among strangers and traveling so far. Rosemary was smiling and gracious as always, and their children and ours hit it off together right away and ran off to play.

The home-cooked meal smelled so good after train fare and sandwiches. As we all sat around the big table in the kitchen, enjoying Rosemary's country cooking, talking, and reminiscing, I looked at each face around the table. My heart overflowed with gratitude and love.

(A Joyous Heart, 147-148*)*

Porky Pie

4 med. sweet potatoes	1 lb. ground pork
1 1/2 t. salt	1 1/2 c. water
2 T. butter	2 T. flour
1 1/2 t. cinnamon sugar	Dash of pepper

Cook potatoes in water with 1 teaspoon of salt, then peel. Mash slightly and add butter, cinnamon sugar, and remaining salt. Add a little milk if necessary. Form pork into patties; brown them and drain. Make gravy with pork broth, water, flour, and pepper. Pour over patties in shallow baking pan. Spread sweet potatoes on top, and bake at 400° for 20 minutes.

Washday Dinner

Melt 1 tablespoon butter in large casserole dish. Line bottom with thick layer of onions, then add generous layer of potatoes. Over potatoes, sprinkle 2 tablespoons flour and pour can (1 pt.) of tomato juice. Cover top with thinly sliced sausages, and add boiling water to cover all ingredients. Add salt to taste. Bake at 300° for 3 hours. If sausages get too brown, turn them over.

Feeling relief, Nancy realized that Mary was still the same sister she always was. "Do come in!" Mary cried happily. "You're just in time to help me get dinner ready for the threshing crew. The threshing rig came this morning."

Mary listened hungrily to each morsel of news about the family at home. She was only twenty-one, and this was her first year of marriage. Although she would never admit it, and least of all to Jacob, she was homesick at times. But having Nancy here would help that.

While preparing the dinner, the sisters chatted as fast as they worked. Finally it was nearly ready. Nancy grated the cabbage for slaw and set the long table. The meat loaf was browned to perfection. Nancy and Mary took turns thumping the big potato masher in the kettle to make *gschtammde Grummbiere* (mashed potatoes). After they all bowed their heads for a silent grace, the eating began.

"Pass the *gschtammde Grummbiere*," Mary told Nancy, as she walked by with two platters of meat loaf.

Quickly Nancy passed the mashed potatoes and one dish after the other, as fast as the men were ready for them. It took a lot of food to feed so many hardworking men!

(*Summerville Days*, 15-19)

Savory Meat Loaf

1 1/4 lbs. ground beef plus	1 beaten egg
1/4 lb. ground pork OR	1/4 t. pepper
2 lbs. ground beef	1 t. mustard
1/4 c. minced onions	1/4 c. ketchup
1 c. oatmeal or crushed crackers	1 c. tomato juice
2 1/2 t. salt	Bacon slices

Mix all ingredients, and form mixture into loaf. Put a few bacon slices on top, and pour additional tomato juice over all. Bake at 350° to 375° for 1 hour.

Variations: 1. Press mixture into cake pan, and top with ketchup. Bake for about 1 hour; 2. Spread the following glaze over the loaf: ½ cup brown sugar, 1½ teaspoons prepared mustard, 1 tablespoon Worcestershire sauce (mix together, and add enough vinegar to make a paste).

Beef Roast

3-lb. roast	2 t. brown sugar
2 t. salt	3 T. water (approx.)
Pepper	

Mix together salt, small amount of pepper, and brown sugar, and rub well into all sides of meat. Place meat in casserole dish, and add small amount of water. Roast, covered, at 325° for 1 hour, or until done.

Delicious One-Dish Dinner

Peel, wash, and slice potatoes. Grease casserole dish with butter, and put in layer of potatoes. Add layer of carrots if you wish, then layer of sliced onions. Season with salt and pepper, and put dices of butter on top. Prepare hamburger patties and lay on top. Add a little water and cover casserole with aluminum foil. Bake for 1 hour at 350°.

Variations: 1. Use ham instead of hamburger; 2. Add turnips; 3. Pour diluted (half water) canned tomato soup over casserole.

Poor Man's Steak

1 lb. hamburger	1 c. cracker crumbs
1 c. milk	1 t. salt
¼ t. pepper	1 small onion, finely
1 can (10 oz.) cream	chopped
of mushroom soup	

Mix ingredients and shape mixture into narrow loaf. Let sit for at least 8 hours, or overnight. Slice and fry until brown. Put slices in layers in roaster, and spread mushroom soup on each piece. Bake for 1 hour at 325°.

As we quilted, Priscilla was talking away at a great rate, jumping from one subject to the next. "Did you hear about the midwife that's starting to do home deliveries in this area? I think I'd like to try her next time."

"No, I hadn't heard. I guess I sort of grew out of that. I won't be needing a midwife anymore."

"Don't talk too soon," Priscilla teased, "You're not forty-nine yet. Didn't you hear about Abner Emma [Abner's wife]? She's forty-nine and due in January."

"But she has four grandchildren already! Surely that's not true!"

The day passed quickly with such chatter, for Priscilla kept a conversation going constantly, maybe to keep me from talking about something she didn't want to hear. She served a casserole dish of *Yummasetti* for lunch, and for dessert we had cherry cream cheese delight. Both were delicious!

(A Joyous Heart, 76-77)

Yummasetti

1 large pkg. noodles, cooked in salted water
3 lbs. hamburger, fried in butter with 1 chopped onion
1 pt. peas
1 c. sour cream
2 cans (10 oz. each) cream of mushroom soup
1 can (10 oz.) cream of chicken OR cream of celery soup
1/2 loaf toasted, buttered bread crumbs

Mix together all ingredients (reserving some of bread crumbs) and pour mixture into greased baking dish. Top with reserved crumbs. Bake at 350° for 1 hour.

The leaves will be turning brilliant with rich scarlet and warm gold and dull brown. After the work is done, fall is a good time of year. The cellars and barns and silos are filled, the harvest is over, and we count our blessings and remember to thank God for his goodness.

On Saturday evening we had our neighborhood farewell gathering here for Gloria and George before they start for Arizona. Rudys were here, and Pam, Grandpa Daves and Eli's family, and Martha and Chad.

Barbianne wanted to make part of the meal, so I let her make a haystack supper, something that is becoming quite popular among our people. I'll copy the recipe here so I won't forget it.

(*A Golden Sunbeam*, 156)

Hay Stack

Ritz crackers
Cooked rice
Corn chips OR tortilla chips
Lettuce and shredded carrots
Cheese sauce
Hamburger, plus onions to taste
Taco sauce
Tomatoes, cut up

Cook rice. Crush crackers and corn chips. Brown hamburger and onions. Add taco sauce and chunked tomatoes. Cut up lettuce. To serve, each person takes a plate, and piles items on top of each other—first crackers, then rice, then corn chips, lettuce and carrots, and hamburger mixture. When done, pour cheese sauce over entire stack. Delicious!

"It's so good to be home." Dad thumped his suitcase on the floor and stretched out on the rocker. Lydia ran to him and tried to climb on his knee. He swung her up affectionately.

"Supper's almost ready." Mom's cheeks were pink and flushed from working over the cookstove. "Here, Nancy, you can make the salad." They were preparing Dad's favorite foods: roast chicken garnished with watercress, fresh hot rolls, mashed potatoes, sugar peas, new lettuce out of the hot bed, and shoofly pie.

"Mmmm, all my favorites, and fresh meadow tea yet." Dad was grateful. "I sure missed your good cooking, Mamm."

(Whispering Brook Farm, 219)

Roast Chicken

41/2 lb. hen	Melted butter
1 T. salt	Bread dressing
11/2 t. ginger (opt.)	1 T. flour
1/2 c. water	

Rub inside of chicken with 1½ teaspoons salt (and ginger, if desired). Stuff with bread dressing. (To keep dressing from coming out as chicken roasts, lay a bread crust over dressing before trussing.) Rub outside of chicken with melted butter and sprinkle with remaining salt, to which one tablespoon flour has been added. Place in roasting pan and add water. Do not cover. Roast at 350° for about 21/4 hours, basting with hot drippings every 20 to 25 minutes. (For first part of roasting period, place chicken breast side down, then turn breast side up.) To test for doneness, insert sharp fork into thickest part of breast or thigh. When done, fork will turn easily, and juice will show no trace of red.

Bread dressing:

1 qt. soft bread crumbs	1 t. minced onion
3 eggs	1 t. salt
2 c. milk	1 t. sage OR poultry seasoning
1 T. chopped parsley	2 T. butter OR chicken fat

Beat eggs and add milk; pour over bread crumbs. Add melted fat, parsley, onion, and seasoning, and mix well.

Being at a quilting is a good way to get to know the neighborhood women and also to find out all kinds of gossip—news, I should say. Polly had two quilts in frames. I was there early and didn't see who gathered around the other quilt in the next room. I was wondering so much whether Priscilla was there.

At lunchtime Polly called us to a luscious dinner of fried chicken, mashed potatoes and gravy, homemade noodles, succotash, lettuce salad, ice-cream pie with strawberry topping, and chiffon marble cake.

(A Fruitful Vine, 22)

Crunchy Chicken

3 to 4 lb. cut-up broiler	Melted butter OR margarine
Cracker crumbs	Cornflake crumbs
Salt	Poultry seasonings to taste

Dip pieces of raw chicken into melted butter, then roll in finely crushed equal parts cracker and cornflake crumbs. Place coated chicken in flat, well-greased baking pans, laying pieces side by side without crowding. Sprinkle with salt and your favorite chicken seasonings. Bake at 375° for 1 hour, or until browned and tender.

Vegetables

4

Vegetables

April 3

Peter and Crist helped me drop the seeds into the neat furrows and cover them with rich, dark soil. For some reason I felt more lighthearted and joyous than I had for a long time. I just felt in my bones that perhaps I could still persuade Dora to stay with us.

So I worked happily with the boys, planting peas, potatoes, onions, cabbage, lettuce, parsley, and red beets. Meanwhile, the song sparrows and robins sang with joyous abandon. Peter and Crist each wanted a little garden of their own, so I helped them plan that. Then we planted a row of bright-faced pansies along the edge of the garden.

(A Golden Sunbeam, 78)

Sour Cream Cabbage

4 c. finely grated cabbage	2 T. sour cream
1 T. flour	Salt and pepper

Simmer cabbage until soft in tightly covered saucepan, with very little water. With flour shaker, sprinkle approximately 1 tablespoon flour over cabbage. Add sour cream, and salt and pepper to taste.

Spiced Cabbage

1 tart apple	1/4 t. pepper
6 c. shredded cabbage	1/2 t. celery salt
3 T. butter	1/3 c. water
6 whole cloves	2 T. sugar
2 1/2 t. salt	1/4 c. vinegar

Chop peeled apple coarsely; combine with other ingredients.
Place in greased, deep 2-quart casserole. Cook, covered, in 350°
oven for 1 hour.

Creamed Onions

Cook quartered medium-sized onions in water until tender, about
15 to 25 minutes, depending on age. Add salt, butter, and a paste
of milk and flour to thicken.

New Peas and Potatoes

3 c. fresh peas	1½ c. milk
12 small new potatoes	1½ t. flour
1½ t. salt	2 T. butter

Cook peas and potatoes separately in salted water until soft and
almost dry. Add peas to potatoes and pour milk over them. Bring
milk to boiling point, then add paste of butter and flour. Cook
until slightly thickened, and serve. (This is a good way to stretch
the first peas from the garden.)

The dinner bell was ringing, and Dad and the boys came in from the field. The first thing everyone saw, when they entered the kitchen, was the platter of steaming ears of corn on the cob.

"Whoopee!" Henry shouted. "*Rooschtniers* (roasting ears)!"

"My, sweet corn already!" Dad marveled. "We've never had any this early before. What kind is it?"

"It's new," Mom answered. "Super Early Gold. I hope it tastes as good as it looks."

Nancy felt a stab of guilt as she took the first luscious bite of sweet corn. She remembered how, at first, after Daadi had died, she thought she would never be hungry again or enjoy good food. But then she recalled her talk with Mamm. Smiling, she sank her teeth into the corn on the cob. It was all right. Life was good.

(*Whispering Brook Farm*, 180)

Corn Fritters

6 big ears of corn	Pepper to taste
2 eggs	1 c. flour
1/2 t. salt	1 c. milk

Cut kernels off corn and add rest of ingredients. Mix well, and drop by tablespoons into a frying pan with melted butter or margarine. Turn as with pancakes.

Scalloped Corn

2 c. cooked (or canned) corn	1/8 t. pepper
1 c. milk	1 T. sugar
2/3 c. cracker or bread crumbs	2 eggs
3 T. melted butter	1 t. minced onion
1/2 t. salt	

Beat eggs, and add milk and crumbs. Add corn, onion, seasoning, and melted butter. Mix well, and pour into greased casserole. Bake at 350° for 40 minutes.

After a good refreshing rain last night, the corn in the fields is growing by leaps and bounds. The old saying calls for it to be "knee high by the fourth of July," but it's closer to waist high this year.

Today we had our first meal of sweet corn from the garden. Mmmm, was it ever delicious! Now I can hardly wait for those delicious ripe tomatoes and new lima beans and potatoes. Fresh raspberries, crisp head lettuce, and cabbage are also on the menu.

City folks who can't have a garden sure miss a lot. What one buys at the grocery stores can't begin to compare with the fresh produce straight out of the garden.

(*A Golden Sunbeam,* 152-153)

Creamed Limas

1 quart fresh lima beans	2 T. butter
2 t. salt	1/8 t. pepper
1 1/2 t. sugar	1 c. milk
1 1/2 t. flour	1/4 c. cream

Cover beans with water and cook until tender and almost dry. Add seasoning and milk. When milk has come to a boil, add a paste made with flour and cream. Cook until thickened (2 minutes).

Succotash (*Miriam's Recipe*)

Cook approximately 1 cup lima beans with 4 cups corn, 1 teaspoon salt, and a bit of butter. Add a bit of milk just before serving.

Isaac brought in an armload of sweet corn today, and the tomatoes will soon be ripe. We're already eating new potatoes, and I can hardly wait until the lima beans are ready. Such delicious garden goodies, abundant blessings! May we not forget to thank the Giver.

(*A Fruitful Vine,* 57)

Tomato Casserole

Raw tomatoes, peeled	Salt
Green pepper rings	Pepper
Onion rings	Bread crumbs
Sugar	Butter

Slice tomatoes and place in cake pan. Arrange pepper rings and onion rings over tomatoes, and season with sugar, salt, and pepper. Prepare bread crumbs as for stuffing, seasoning with salt, pepper, and butter; cover vegetables with crumbs. Bake in 350° oven for 1 to 1½ hours.

Tomato Bread

1 qt. tomato juice OR whole tomatoes
Sugar
Pepper
Butter

Heat tomato juice, adding sugar and pepper to taste. Add a lump of butter. Pour over broken toast or soda crackers just before serving.

Fried New Potatoes

1 qt. new potatoes
1 onion
2 T. oil

Grate unpeeled potatoes, slice in onion, and fry together in oil.

The last day of school. We had our annual end-of-the-year school picnic for the parents and school-age and preschool children. Each family brought a hot covered dish and a cold one.

Since we had too much to carry with my big roast pan of scalloped potatoes, Nate hitched the workhorses to the wagon. The children clambered happily on back, and we started off.

The morning was beautiful and cool, with bobwhites calling from the meadows and the sweet fragrance of dewy clover fields wafting on the breeze.

(*A Golden Sunbeam*, 83)

Scalloped Potatoes

6 c. raw potatoes, sliced thin
4 T. flour
2 1/2 t. salt
1/8 t. pepper

1 onion, minced
2 1/2 c. hot milk
2 T. butter

Place layer of potatoes in buttered baking dish. Add minced onion. Sprinkle with salt, pepper, and flour, and dot with butter. Repeat until all ingredients are used. Pour hot milk over potatoes and bake at 350° for 1 to 1 1/4 hours. Serves 6.

Potato Puffs

3 c. mashed potatoes
1 c. hot milk
2 eggs, separated

1 t. salt
1 1/2 T. butter
1/4 c. grated cheese

Add beaten egg yolks to mashed potatoes. Then add salt, parsley, and milk; mix. Fold in stiffly beaten egg whites. Drop by spoonfuls into flat buttered baking dish, placing cakes 1 inch apart. (Greased muffin tins may also be used.) Sprinkle with grated cheese and bake at 400° for 20 minutes.

Soups and Salads

5

Soups and Salads

April 25

Dora and I spent the day at Nate's house. Barbara was there helping, too. This forenoon we planted the garden, digging in the rich, black earth, dropping the seeds, and covering them.

Planting always gives me an awesome feeling of being in company with God. Each seed is a miracle about to unfold! Again, just as we finished, a gentle spring rain began to fall. What a satisfied feeling to know we got the seed in before it rained!

We sat down to a simple meal of vegetable soup and sandwiches, then walked through the house, inspecting everything.

(*A Fruitful Vine,* 149-150)

Vegetable Soup

1 large soup bone
  OR ribs of beef
2 c. diced potatoes
2 large onions, diced
1 c. shredded cabbage
4 ripe tomatoes
3 large carrots, sliced
1/2 stalk celery
1/2 can whole corn
  OR 4 ears corn

1/2 pt. string beans, cut finely
1 green pepper, diced
1 red pepper, diced
1 c. lima beans
1 c. peas OR sugar peas, in season
1/8 c. rice
1/4 c. barley
parsley leaves

Cook soup bone or meat in water to cover, until half done. Add raw vegetables and cook for 1/2 hour; then add cooked vegetables; simmer until all ingredients are well done. Cook rice and barley separately, or put in kettle with meat at the beginning. Add chili powder to make soup more tasty.

Succotash Chowder

1 large onion, chopped
3 T. butter
1 c. fresh OR canned corn
1 c. fresh OR canned lima beans
2 c. potatoes, diced
1 c. water

1 t. salt
1/4 t. pepper
1 t. parsley, chopped
3 c. milk
2 T. flour
1/4 c. water

Sauté onion in butter in a pressure cooker until onion is slightly browned. Add vegetables, 1 cup of water, salt, and pepper. Cover, and begin cooking. When pressure control jiggles, cook for 2 minutes, then reduce pressure immediately. Add milk and heat to boiling. Blend flour with 1/4 cup water to make a smooth paste, then add to soup cooking it for 1 minute while stirring constantly. Garnish servings with chopped parsley.

Onion Tomato Soup

1/2 medium-sized onion, cut up	Water
Celery leaves, dried or fresh	Sugar
4 T. butter or margarine	Salt
1/2 c. flour (approx.)	Red pepper OR paprika
Tomato juice (about 4 c.)	Cream OR milk

Sauté onion and celery leaves in butter. When onion is tender, stir in flour till slightly browned, then slowly add tomato juice. Stir mixture until smooth and the thickness of gravy. Add water, sugar, salt, and red pepper or paprika to taste. Before serving, add some cream or milk.

October 20

Today was a most lovely October day, with sunshine and blue skies, clear and crisp, with a sweeping wind—the kind of weather that makes us glad to be alive. We all piled on the spring wagon and drove up the old woods road to gather bushels of hickory nuts and black walnuts.

The trees along the creek were gorgeous with leaves of vibrant yellow, rich red, and warm gold. The air was mellow and tangy with the scent of decaying leaves and old wood smoke, and the pungent, indescribable aromas of autumn.

At lunch time we built a fire to heat our big kettle of vegetable soup. On a tablecloth, we spread our lunch of soup, bologna sandwiches, chowchow, cookies, and a jug of cider. It's not hard to figure out why the meal tastes so much better out in the woodsy autumn splendor, with crinkled brown leaves floating gently down around us. The food took on the flavor of autumn sunshine and scents and breezes.

(A Golden Sunbeam, 106)

Old-Fashioned Bean Soup and Ham

1 lb. dry navy beans
1 ham bone (or bacon)
3 qt. water
1/2 c. chopped green pepper
1 c. celery, chopped
2 c. diced potatoes

1 medium onion,
   chopped
3 carrots, sliced
1 T. salt
1/4 t. pepper
1 c. tomato juice

Simmer beans and the ham bone in water for 2 hours. Add rest of ingredients and simmer for 2 hours longer, or until beans are tender. (Soaking beans ahead of time will cut down on cooking time.)

Potato Cream Soup

2 c. raw potatoes, diced
2 onions, minced
2 stalks diced celery OR
   2 T. dried celery leaves
2 1/2 c. boiling water

1 T. butter
3 1/2 T. flour
2 c. milk
1 1/2 t. salt
1/4 t. pepper

Cook potatoes, onions, and celery in boiling water. Melt butter, and add flour, milk, and seasoning to make a white sauce. Cook until thick and smooth. Rub potato mixture through a sieve, add white sauce and garnish with parsley before serving. Serve with crackers.

Hearty Hamburger Soup

2 T. butter
1 lb. ground beef
1 c. chopped onions
1 c. sliced carrots
1/2 c. chopped green peppers
2 c. tomato juice

1 c. diced potatoes
1 1/2 t. salt
1 t. seasoned salt
1/8 t. pepper
1/3 c. flour
4 c. milk

Melt butter in saucepan and brown meat. Add onions and cook until transparent. Stir in remaining ingredients, except for flour and milk. Cover and cook over low heat till vegetables are tender, 20 to 25 minutes. Combine flour with 1 cup of milk, and stir into soup mixture. Bring to a boil, add remaining milk, and heat through, stirring frequently. (Do not boil after remaining milk is added.)

Cream of Corn Soup

2 c. boiling water	2 c. milk
2 c. canned OR cooked corn	2 T. butter
1/2 c. celery, chopped	2 T. flour
1 T. onion, chopped	1 t. salt
1/2 c. parsley, chopped	1/8 t. pepper

Add corn, celery, onion, and parsley to boiling water, cover and simmer for 20 minutes, then drain liquid into another pan. Scald milk and add to corn stock. Melt butter and mix with flour before adding to combined liquids. Add vegetables to the liquids. Season and heat mixture to boiling point.

On Wednesday afternoon Mom sent Nancy back to the spring for fresh watercress. They were hoping Dad would be home in time for supper, and watercress was one of his favorites. Nancy walked the half mile through the buttercup-filled meadow to the big tree where the spring flowed out of the ground and on down into Whispering Brook.

It was all so dear and beautiful—the lush green meadow grass, and the new leaves on the trees. She waded into the spring with her boots on, carefully cut off the tender green cress, and filled her bag with it.

(*Whispering Brook Farm*, 218)

Dressing for Greens

Bacon	Vinegar
1 T. flour	Sour cream OR buttermilk
1 c. water	2 hardcooked eggs, diced
1 T. sugar	Greens
Salt	

Cut up a few strips of bacon and fry. Stir flour into part of drippings. When brown, stir in water and let boil before adding sugar, salt, and vinegar to taste. A bit of sour cream or buttermilk may be added. Fold in hardcooked eggs. Add greens just before serving. This dressing is good with dandelions, lettuce, endive, and other greens.

Summer Salad

Take several tablespoons of olive oil, cooking oil, or sour cream. Add vinegar or lemon juice, then salt to taste. For a sweet salad, mix honey or sugar with oil. Add ½ banana, finely diced. After making dressing, add any of the following vegetables (or others of your choice):

Lettuce	Carrots
Radishes	Tomatoes
Cucumber	Onions
Celery	Spinach

Mix thoroughly, then add 1 handful raisins and 1 handful crushed peanuts (optional).

Variations: For simpler salad, try using only lettuce and onions, or lettuce and diced apples.

May 12

Beautiful blossom time! The lilac bush is laden with fragrant lavender bouquets. The fruit trees are in various stages, each with their own special beauty and fragrance.

A cardinal is singing from the pine tree these days. His "pretty, pretty, pretty," then "good cheer, good cheer, good cheer" is a welcome part of the bird chorus in the morning. I hope they build a nest there.

The garden is as pretty as a picture. Leaf lettuce and radishes are ready. Maybe next week the carrots will be big enough to start using them as we thin out the rows. The peas look nice, and also the potatoes. I hope I can keep the garden as weedfree all summer as it is now.

(*A Golden Sunbeam*, 141)

Carrot Salad

1 pkg. (3 oz.) orange gelatin   2 T. sugar (opt.)
1/2 c. carrots, finely grated   Raisins (opt.)
1 c. crushed pineapple

Prepare gelatin according to directions on box, using slightly more water. When gelatin starts to thicken, add carrots and pineapple. For a sweeter salad, add sugar, and add raisins according to taste. Stir and let set.

Pea Salad

1 c. cooked peas   1/2 c. sweet pickles, chopped
1 c. celery, finely cut   1/2 c. diced cheese

Season ingredients with salt, pepper, and sugar, and mix with mayonnaise.

Green Bean Salad

1 lb. green beans   1/3 c. vinegar
2 small onions   21/2 T. sugar
6 slices bacon   1/2 t. salt

Wash green beans and cut off and discard ends. Cut beans into 1-inch pieces. Cook for 15 to 20 minutes, or until tender. Drain thoroughly and put into bowl, keeping them warm. Meanwhile, clean onions and cut into 1/8-inch thick slices. Separate slices into rings, and put in bowl with beans.

Dice and fry bacon until crisp, without pouring off drippings. Add vinegar, sugar, and salt. Heat this mixture to boiling, stirring well. Pour bacon/vinegar mixture over beans and onions, tossing lightly to coat thoroughly.

Potato Salad

1 qt. cooked, salted, diced potatoes
2 c. Velvet Salad Dressing
10 (or fewer) hardcooked eggs, sliced
1 small onion, minced
1/2 c. celery, finely chopped (opt.)

Mix ingredients and serve.

Velvet Salad Dressing

1 egg	1 t. prepared mustard
1 T. flour	4 T. vinegar
½ c. sugar	1 c. cold water
1 t. salt	3 T. butter

Beat egg well, then add flour, sugar, salt, mustard, vinegar, and water. Cook in double boiler until thick. Remove from heat and beat in butter. This dressing is good on lettuce or potato salads. Cream or 2 tablespoons mayonnaise may be added.

Sadie's Salad Dressing

1/4 c. vinegar	1/3 c. catsup
1/4 c. cooking oil	1/4 c. sugar (or less)
1 T. minced onion	1/3 c. salad dressing OR
1/2 t. salt	mayonnaise

Mix and shake well. Will keep a while in refrigerator. This is good over Buttercrunch lettuce and a chopped tomato. Add ½ cup cubed cheese, if desired.

Pies

6

Pies

June 12

These last few weeks have been busy with peas and strawberries. This afternoon I made a luscious strawberry pie topped with whipped cream, and now I can hardly wait to surprise Isaac.

He's busy with the hay, and if I wouldn't be so busy myself, I'd love to help, too. There is a warm, fragrant south wind blowing over the new-mown hay fields, and the sweet fragrance of the rambler roses on the trellis floats in through the open kitchen window. "What is so rare as a day in June?" (J. R. Lowell).

(A Fruitful Vine, 53)

Strawberry Pie

1 1/2 qt. fresh strawberries
2 c. sugar
1/2 c. cornstarch

Combine strawberries and sugar, and let stand for 2 hours. Drain off juice and add water to make 2 cups. Blend in cornstarch and cook over low heat until mixture is thickened. Mix with strawberries and let cool. Pour into baked pie crust or graham cracker crust, and serve with whipped cream.

Blueberry Pie

4 c. fresh blueberries   1/3 c. flour
1 c. sugar   1/2 t. cinnamon

Mix sugar, flour, and cinnamon, and mix lightly through berries. Pour into pastry-lined pan, and cover with top crust. Bake at 400° for 50 minutes, or until crust is nicely browned and juice bubbles through slits in crust.

August 27

This forenoon, at my request, Nate got the old boat down. We loaded it with empty boxes and baskets and headed upstream looking for elderberries. They grow on bushes along the banks and can be picked from the boat.

What a lot of memories came flooding back! There was the time I was going boating with Nate before we were married.

We talked and reminisced about those pretending-courtship days as we picked the juicy purple berries. A few late summer birds were chirping in the trees, and it was so peaceful and serene there on the water.

After we had filled our containers, we headed back, refreshed by the beauty and calmness of nature. Priscilla and I had a busy day ahead, canning *Hollerbier* (elderberry) juice and making *Hollerbier* jelly and pies. Mmmmm! What tastes better?

(*A Winding Path*, 91-92)

Elderberry Custard Pie

1 c. elderberry juice   1/4 t. salt
4 T. flour   1 egg, separated
1 c. sugar   1 c. milk

Bring elderberry juice to a boil. Combine flour, sugar, and salt, then gradually add egg yolk and milk. Add this mixture to boiling juice and stir until it thickens. Fold in stiffly beaten egg white. Pour mixture into unbaked pie shell, and bake at 350° for 20 to 30 minutes.

Cherry Pie

2 T. tapioca	1/2 c. cherry juice
1/8 t. salt	1/4 t. almond extract
1 c. sugar	Red food coloring (opt.)
3 c. drained, pitted	
sour cherries	

Mix ingredients and let mixture stand for 15 minutes. Pour into 9-inch pie shell, and dot with 1 tablespoon butter. Add top crust, and bake at 425° for 50 minutes.

December 16

Grandma has some decided opinions on what one should eat and what to avoid.

She says it would be all right if we'd eat the whole sugar beet, fiber and all, the way God made it. But to refine the sugar out and add it to food, that's unhealthy, not God's will. And the flours—they're all right if from whole grain, but not if milled and the wheat germ and outer husk removed. Therefore, white flour is a no-no.

Yesterday Allen went to the grocery store and bought a bag of sugar and a bag of white flour. He carried them in with the other groceries, and before he went out the door, he said in a low voice, so Grandma wouldn't hear, "Make some apple pies this afternoon." . . .

Fortunately, Grandma went to her room for her nap. When she came out, the kitchen was filled with the wonderful aroma of freshly baked apple pies. She walked over to inspect them. I had prepared myself to 'see her pinching her mouth shut and sulking the rest of the day, or giving me a scolding.

But Grandma wouldn't do that. She smiled and said, "My, these pies smell good. You did the right thing in making them when Allen asked you to."

So she *had* heard! "I suppose everyone has to learn the hard way," she added sadly, "like I did."

At suppertime when I carried a pie to the table, I was greeted by cheers from the family, and two whole pies disappeared fast.

(*A Fruitful Vine*, 78-79)

Apple Pie

2 T. flour
6 medium apples, sliced
1 c. sugar

1/4 t. cinnamon
1 T. water
1 t. butter

Mix flour, apples, sugar, and cinnamon. Pour into unbaked pie shell, add water, and dot center with butter. Place 1/2-inch strips of dough lattice-style over apples, connecting strips to sides of pie shell. Bake at 400° until apples are done.

Dutch Apple Pie

3 c. sliced apples
1 c. sugar
3 T. flour
1/2 t. cinnamon
1 beaten egg

1 c. light cream
1 t. vanilla
1/2 c. chopped nuts
1 T. butter

Place apples in 9-inch unbaked pie shell. Mix together sugar, flour, and cinnamon. Combine egg, cream, and vanilla; add sugar mixture, mixing well. Pour over apples, then sprinkle with nuts and dot with butter. Bake pie at 350° for 45 to 50 minutes, until apples are tender.

June 16

Today I thoroughly cleaned the entire kitchen. I scrubbed, polished, and waxed until everything shone. Then I got out my rolling pin and flour, sugar, and some more of Grandma's no-no's, and made five delicious raspberry pies. Since Grandma is gone, the family is regularly demanding pies, cookies, and desserts.

(*A Fruitful Vine*, 98)

Miriam's Black Raspberry Cream Pie

2 c. black raspberries   1 c. cream
3/4 c. sugar   1 t. vanilla
3 T. flour

Sprinkle raspberries in 8-inch unbaked pie shell. Mix sugar and flour and sprinkle over raspberries. Combine cream and vanilla, and pour over all. Bake at 350° until done (about 45 minutes).

April 4

Today I made fifteen *Schnitz-boi* (dried-apple pies), with little Crist's help. Rudy and Barbianne are having church at their house tomorrow, and I decided to make some of the pies here to help them out.

It takes me twice as long to do things with Crist, but I don't want to discourage his helpfulness. He wants a turn with the rolling pin, to be the one to add the sugar and cinnamon, to taste it for sweetness (the best part), and to crimp the edges.

(*A Treasured Friendship*, 132)

Dried Schnitz Pie

2 c. dried tart apples   1/4 t. powdered cloves
2/3 c. sugar   1/2 t. cinnamon
11/2 c. water   Pastry for 2 (9-inch) crusts

Soak apples in 11/2 cups of warm water, then cook in the same water until soft. Rub apples through colander, and add sugar and spices. Put mixture in unbaked pie shell, and cover with top crust. Bake at 425° for 15 minutes. Reduce temperature to 375° and bake for 35 minutes more.

Half-Moon Pies

1 qt. apple *Schnitz* (dried pieces)
1 1/2 c. water
1 qt. applesauce

1 1/2 c. brown sugar
1/2 t. cinnamon
1/2 t. salt

To make filling, boil apple *Schnitz* in water till water is absorbed and *Schnitz* is soft. Drain in colander. Add to applesauce, sugar, cinnamon, and salt. Make pie crust dough, and shape a piece the size of an egg for each pie. Roll out thinly, and fold dough over to make a crease through the center. Unfold, and make 2 holes in top part. On other half of dough circle, place 1/2 cup of filling. Wet edges of dough and fold over, pressing edges together. Cut off remaining dough with pie crimper. Brush top with buttermilk or beaten egg, and bake at 450° until brown.

October 17

Saturday. We gathered all the large orange pumpkins and the tiny jack-be-littles and the green-and-white striped-neck pumpkins for pies. The golden maple leaves are falling everywhere. We rake them into huge piles. The children love to jump around in them.

The crisp air and outdoor exercise sure works up an appetite. When the wind became chilly, we were all glad to be going in to supper fires and good things to eat.

(A Golden Sunbeam, 30)

Pumpkin Pie

1 1/2 c. cooked pumpkin
1 c. brown sugar
1 1/2 c. milk
3 eggs, separated
1/2 t. salt

1 T. cornstarch
1/4 t. ginger
1/4 t. cloves
1 t. cinnamon

Cook and mash pumpkin, and add beaten egg yolks, sugar, and spices. Add milk and mix thoroughly. Fold in stiffly beaten egg whites. Pour mixture into unbaked crust. Bake at 425° for 10 minutes, then reduce heat to 350° and bake for 30 minutes.

Bob Andy Pie

2 c. brown OR white sugar	1 T. butter
4 T. flour	3 eggs, separated
1/2 t. cloves	2 c. milk
1 t. cinnamon	

Mix dry ingredients, then add butter, beaten egg yolks, and milk. Fold in beaten egg whites. Pour mixture into 2 unbaked pie crusts and bake at 400° for 10 minutes, then at 350° until done.

March 5

Last evening I was puttering around the kitchen rather late, doing some baking after the children and Rudy were in bed, when someone knocked insistently on the wash-house door. My first impulse was to flee up the stairs and wake Rudy, and I started for the stair door, heart beating wildly.

Yet something made me turn around and unlock the door, and there stood Nate, suitcase in hand, smiling broadly! I welcomed him joyously.

"I'm hungry as a bear," Nate declared, sniffing the air. "What smells so good? I haven't had any lunch nor supper. The van broke down just outside of town, and I walked the rest of the way home."

So I quickly heated some soup, made a few sandwiches for him, and took the shoofly pies out of the oven. After Nate had eaten, we sat and talked until midnight. The March winds howling outside suddenly were friendly again, the house-creaking sounds were dear and familiar.

(*A Joyous Heart*, 17-18)

Gooey Shoofly Pie

Make crumbs by mixing the following ingredients:

2 c. flour   1/2 t. nutmeg (opt.)
3/4 c. brown sugar   1 t. cinnamon (opt.)
1/3 c. shortening OR butter

To make the syrup, combine the following:

1 c. molasses   1 c. hot water
1/2 c. brown sugar   1 t. soda, dissolved in
2 eggs   hot water

Have ready 2 unbaked pie shells. Pour one-fourth of syrup into each pie crust, then add one-fourth of crumbs. Repeat. Bake pie for 10 minutes at 400°, then reduce heat to 350° for 50 minutes. Makes 2 pies.

Cakes

7

Cakes

We were invited to Ben Esh's for supper tonight. I was glad because it would be an excellent opportunity for Isaac to notice Rosemary, I thought. Hmmm, no other guests! A delicious supper. Wonderful fellowship. They are dear, good people.

Then, surprise of surprises, Rosemary carried in a big, beautifully decorated birthday cake with candles. Everyone sang, "Happy birthday to you, Happy birthday to you, Happy birthday, dear Miriam, Happy birthday to you!"

I was simply struck dumb. Matthew clapped his hands and laughed gleefully and said, "Mammie, cakie."

Everyone burst out laughing at that.

"How did you know?" I finally managed to ask. "I never told a single soul it's my birthday."

Rosemary blushed and said, "A little bird told me."
(A Fruitful Vine, 54)

Lemon Layer Cake

2/3 c. butter	3 c. cake flour
13/4 c. sugar	21/2 t. baking powder
2 eggs	1/2 t. salt
11/2 t. vanilla	11/4 c. milk

Cream butter and sugar. Add eggs and vanilla and beat until fluffy. Mix flour, baking powder, and salt, and add alternately with milk to egg mixture, beating after each addition. Beat batter thoroughly before pouring into 2 greased and floured 9-inch round pans. Bake at 350° for 30 to 35 minutes. Allow cakes to cool, then remove from pans. Fill cakes with lemon filling (below), and top cake with Fluffy White Frosting (page 74).

Lemon filling:

3/4 c. sugar	2 egg yolks, slightly beaten
2 T. cornstarch	3 T. lemon juice
1/2 t. salt	1 t. grated lemon peel
3/4 c. water	1 T. butter

Combine sugar, cornstarch, and salt in saucepan. Add water, egg yolks, and lemon juice. Cook and stir over medium heat until thick. Remove from heat, and add lemon peel and butter.

Banana Nut Cake

1 c. white sugar	1 t. soda
1/2 c. butter	2 t. baking powder
2 eggs, well-beaten	Pinch of salt
4 T. sour milk	1 t. cream of tartar
1 t. vanilla	1 c. mashed bananas
2 c. flour	1/2 c. chopped nuts

Cream sugar and butter, then add eggs, milk, and vanilla. Add dry ingredients, then bananas and nuts. Bake in greased and floured 9-x-13-inch pan at 375° for 40 minutes or until done.

Oatmeal Cake

1 1/4 c. boiling water	1 1/2 c. cake flour
1 c. quick oats	1 t. nutmeg (opt.)
1/2 c. shortening	1 t. cinnamon
1 c. brown sugar	1 t. soda
1 c. white sugar	1/2 t. salt
2 eggs	1 t. vanilla

Pour boiling water over oatmeal and let sit for 20 minutes. Cream shortening and sugars well. Add unbeaten eggs, one at a time, beating well after each addition. Blend in oatmeal mixture. Fold in flour, spices, soda, and salt, and add vanilla. Bake in greased and floured 9-x-13-inch pan at 350° for 30 to 35 minutes.

While cake is still hot from the oven, spread with the following topping (mixed well), and put under broiler for 2 minutes or until brown:

2/3 c. brown sugar	6 T. melted butter
1 c. chopped nuts	1/4 c. cream
1 c. coconut	1 t. vanilla

Chocolate Mayonnaise Cake

2 c. all-purpose flour	1 c. boiling water
1 c. sugar	1 t. vanilla
1/2 c. cocoa	1 c. mayonnaise
2 t. soda	

Mix all ingredients and bake batter in 2 greased and floured 8-inch layer pans at 350° for 30 minutes.

Grandma and Grandpa were having dinner with them today. When Nancy went into the pantry for a loaf of homemade bread, she saw a large, white, splendidly iced cake, with "Happy Birthday, Daed" on it. So that was behind the celebration! She had forgotten all about today being Daed's birthday.

Mammi and Daadi were seated at the head of the table, and they all bowed their heads to ask a silent blessing on the food. The main topic of conversation was the sign on the barn.

"Whose idea was it, anyway?" Joe wanted to know.

Grandpa caught Nancy's eye and winked broadly. Nancy blushed. She knew that Daadi wouldn't give away her secret. . . .

When Mary carried in the cake and handed it to her dad, the sign was completely forgotten. Everyone joined in singing, "Happy Birthday to You."

Dad beamed his appreciation. "Thanks to every one of you." He cut the cake into generous pieces. "It's nice to be remembered."

Nancy looked at each person around the table as she slowly ate her ice cream, savoring each bite. *It's so nice to have the family all together like this,* she thought. *I wish it could always stay like this, and no one would ever leave home.*

(*Whispering Brook Farm*, 30-31)

Roman Apple Cake

1 c. brown sugar	1/4 t. baking powder
1/2 c. shortening	1/4 t. soda
1 egg	1/4 t. salt
1 t. vanilla	1/2 c. milk
1 1/2 c. all-purpose flour	4 medium apples, chopped

Mix all ingredients except apples, then fold them in.

Topping:

1 T. melted butter	2 t. cinnamon
1/2 c. brown sugar	2 t. flour
1/2 c. chopped nuts	

Mix topping ingredients, and sprinkle mixture as crumbs over the batter. Bake at 350° for 45 minutes. Serve cake warm.

Feather Cake

1/2 c. shortening	3 c. self-rising flour
2 c. sugar	1 t. vanilla
1 c. milk	3 whole eggs OR 5 egg whites

Cream shortening, add sugar, and cream again. Add milk and flour alternately, then add the vanilla. Add eggs last. Mix batter and bake at 350° for 30 to 40 minutes in pans of your choice. *Note: If using all-purpose flour, add 3 teaspoons baking powder and 1/2 teaspoon salt.*

When I came home, Rachel was lying on the sofa, crying heartbrokenly. (Why does she take the difficulties of life, both big and small, with such intense feeling?)

"I wanted to bake you a birthday cake," she sobbed, "and it flopped."

Only then did I notice a rather flat-looking cake on the counter.

"And that Clyde!" she cried reproachfully. "He came in and saw it and asked if I sat on it." More tears and sniffles.

With admirable self-control, I didn't laugh, but told her that she could try again, and I would help her. And so we had a lovely frosted birthday cake for supper, and a happy girl once again. The pigs enjoyed the flopped cake, judging by the speed with which they devoured it.

(*A Fruitful Vine*, 99-100)

Cream Cheese Frosting

| 8 oz. white cream cheese | 1 lb. powdered sugar |
| 8 T. margarine | 2 t. vanilla |

Cream cheese and margarine, then add sugar and vanilla, stirring until creamy.

Fluffy White Frosting

2 egg whites
1/2 c. sugar
1/2 c. white corn syrup

Put egg whites in top of double boiler, and add sugar and corn syrup. Beat mixture over boiling water until thick enough to form stiff peaks when beater is raised. Then spread over cake and swirl it. Icing will stay soft.

Soft Icing

3 T. flour
2/3 c. milk
3/4 c. vegetable shortening

Flavoring
3/4 c. granulated sugar

Cook flour and milk until thick, then let cool. Cream shortening, flavoring of your choice, and sugar. Combine the two mixtures and beat vigorously till icing is smooth.

Creamy Caramel Frosting

4 T. margarine
1 c. brown sugar,
   firmly packed
1/4 t. salt

1/4 c. whole milk
2 1/2 c. powdered sugar
   (approx.)
1/2 t. vanilla

Melt margarine in saucepan. Blend in brown sugar and salt. Cook over low heat, stirring constantly for 2 minutes. Stir in milk, and continue stirring until mixture comes to a boil. Remove from heat and gradually blend in powdered sugar. Add vanilla. If necessary, thin frosting with a small amount of evaporated milk.

Minute Fudge Icing

1/4 c. butter
1 c. sugar

1/4 c. cocoa (scant)
1/4 c. milk

Melt butter in saucepan, then add rest of ingredients. Stir mixture over low heat till all ingredients are dissolved. Bring to a rolling boil, and boil for 1 minute. Remove from heat and beat until creamy enough to spread.

Cookies and Candies

8

Cookies and Candies

September 16

Tonight when Dora came home from school, she flung her bonnet into a corner, raced up the stairs, and slammed the door to her room. The sound of stormy weeping floated downstairs. Wearily, I trudged up the stairs after her, dreading to hear what she had to say.

"I hate school!" She was angry. "The teacher is nice, but it's those stupid children I don't like. They won't play with me, and they called me names." She burst into a fresh round of sobbing.

"Well, change into your everyday clothes and come downstairs. Help me mix chocolate chip cookies, and we'll talk about it."

She told me all about it as she stirred the shortening and sugar and mixed in the eggs with the big wooden spoon. Jimmy, a boy in her class, had called her "the bonnet girl," and soon all the rest were calling her "bonnie girl." She again wiped away a few tears as she told it.

"Don't you know what *bonnie* means?" I asked.

She shook her head no.

"It means 'handsome' or 'pretty,' and I'd be glad if someone called me bonnie."

"Does it really?" Her eyes lit up. "I thought they meant I look like a *Haas* (bunny)."

We laughed together then, and she was her happy self again.

(A Joyous Heart, 70)

Chocolate Chip Cookies

1 c. shortening
3/4 c. brown sugar
3/4 c. white sugar
2 eggs, beaten
1 t. hot water
1 t. vanilla

1 1/2 c. all-purpose flour
1 t. soda
1 t. salt
2 c. oatmeal
1 c. chopped nuts
1 package (12 oz.)
   chocolate chips

Cream shortening, sugars, eggs, hot water, and vanilla. Add flour, soda, and salt. Then mix in oatmeal, nuts, and chocolate chips. Drop batter by teaspoons onto greased cookie sheet, and bake at 350° for 10 to 15 minutes.

Molasses Sugar Cookies

1 c. sugar
3/4 c. shortening
1/4 c. molasses
1 egg
2 c. all-purpose flour

2 t. soda
1 t. cinnamon
1/2 t. cloves
1/2 t. ginger
1/2 t. salt

Cream sugar and shortening. Add molasses and egg; beat well. Stir in dry ingredients, mix well, and chill. Form dough into 1-inch balls and roll in granulated sugar. Place 2 inches apart on greased cookie sheets. Flatten with spoon or fork. Bake at 350° for 8 to 10 minutes. Makes 4 dozen cookies.

At Sol Bylers', benches had been set up in the large shop for the church services. Nancy sat beside Sally and listened to the familiar old slow tunes. Jacob was a *Vorsinger* (song leader), and his rich baritone voice rose and fell in a solo until it was time for the others to join in.

Nancy did not know the preachers here in Summerville. The preacher who had the *Aafang* (shorter, beginning sermon) spoke in a singsong way that made her feel sleepy, and her thoughts began to wander.

My, it was warm! The shop doors were wide open, but hardly a breeze stirred. A bee buzzed in and droned lazily at the window. Nancy glanced over to the bench where Lakisha was sitting. She wondered how the Fresh Air girl was taking it, having to sit so long. And now she couldn't understand a word of what was going on.

Sol Byler Annie came into the shop with snacks to pass around for the younger children: a plate of sugar cookies, graham crackers, and a pitcher of water with cups. This broke the monotony and was a pleasant diversion for them. Lakisha snacked. Nancy, however, decided she was too old for that.

(*Summerville Days*, 59-62)

Miriam's Church Cookies

5 c. sugar	2 t. vanilla
2 1/2 c. shortening	1/2 t. ginger
OR lard	1 c. molasses
1/2 t. cinnamon	1 c. hot water
1 t. baking powder	3 T. soda
1 t. salt	4 eggs
	15 to 18 c. flour

Dissolve soda in cup of hot water. Mix ingredients in order given, to make a soft dough. Roll out on floured surface, cut into shapes and bake at 350° for approximately 10 minutes. Makes 16 dozen large cookies.

Mary's Sugar Cookies

2 eggs
1 1/2 c. granulated sugar
1 c. shortening OR lard
1 t. vanilla
1 c. milk

4 c. all-purpose flour
2 t. baking powder
2 t. cream of tartar
2 t. soda (scant)

Beat eggs for 1 minute. Add sugar and lard, and beat mixture for 1 minute more. Add vanilla and milk, and mix in dry ingredients. Drop by spoonfuls onto cookie sheet and bake at 400° until golden brown. When cool, spread with icing:

6 T. butter (softened)
2 t. vanilla
1/8 t. salt

1 lb. powdered sugar
4 to 5 T. milk

Mix all ingredients and beat for 1 minute. Divide icing into several parts, and color each part with a different food coloring, to add variety to cookies.

The grandparents' kitchen was a cheery place. Geraniums bloomed at the windowsills, the black gas stove sparkled and shone, the walls and ceiling were painted with high-gloss white paint, and on the dry sink stood the familiar blue-and-white washbowl and pitcher set—the very one that Daadi had bought for Mammi when she was a bride.

After her bath, Nancy sat at the kitchen table across from where Daadi sat reading the big German Bible. Mammi poured her a glass of milk from the old-fashioned brown ceramic pitcher and set out a plate of oatmeal raisin cookies.

(*Whispering Brook Farm*, 17)

Oatmeal Raisin Cookies

1 c. raisins	1/2 t. baking powder
1 c. water	1 t. baking soda
3/4 c. shortening	1 t. salt
1 1/2 c. sugar	1 t. cinnamon
2 eggs	1/4 t. ground cloves
1 t. vanilla	2 c. quick oatmeal
2 1/2 c. flour	3/4 c. chopped nuts

Simmer raisins in water for 15 minutes. Drain and reserve liquid, adding more water to make 1/2 cup. Cream shortening and sugar; add eggs and vanilla and beat until fluffy. Add dry ingredients alternately with reserved raisin liquid. Mix oatmeal and nuts with raisins and stir in. Drop by spoonfuls onto greased baking sheet. Bake at 375° for 8 to 10 minutes. Makes 6 to 7 dozen.

Raisin-Filled Cookies

Filling:

2 c. chopped raisins	1 c. sugar
2 T. flour	1 T. lemon juice
1 c. water	

Combine ingredients and boil until mixture is thick.

Dough:

1 c. shortening	2 t. vanilla
2 c. brown sugar	7 c. all-purpose flour
2 eggs	2 t. soda
1 c. milk	2 t. baking powder

Cream shortening, and add sugar gradually. Add well-beaten eggs and beat mixture until smooth. Mix in milk and vanilla. Add dry ingredients and mix well. Roll out dough and cut with round cutter. For each cookie, put 1 teaspoon filling on a circle. Make a hole (with a thimble) in the middle of another circle, and place on top. (Do not press together.) Bake at 350° for 20 minutes or until done.

I should be working outside more, getting more exercise. Just this morning I stepped on the scales and noticed that I have to lose at least ten pounds of what I call "baby fat." Immediately I decided that I simply must go on a diet. Then this afternoon Priscilla baked whoopie pies, and I decided to wait until tomorrow. Sigh!

(*A Winding Path*, 83)

Whoopie Pies

1 1/2 c. butter OR margarine, softened	5 1/2 c. flour
3 c. sugar	1 1/2 t. baking soda
3 eggs	1 1/2 t. salt
2 t. vanilla	2/3 c. cocoa
	2 1/4 c. sour milk OR buttermilk

Cream butter and sugar, add eggs and vanilla, and beat until fluffy. Add dry ingredients alternately with milk. Chill dough at least 1 hour. Drop onto greased baking sheet, and bake at 350° for 8 minutes.

Filling:

2 egg whites	2 T. powdered sugar
2 t. clear vanilla	1 c. shortening
1/4 c. flour	2 1/2 c. powdered sugar
3 T. milk	

Beat together thoroughly egg whites, vanilla, flour, milk, and 2 tablespoons powdered sugar. Add shortening, and 2½ cups powdered sugar, beating until fluffy. Spread between cookies.

Alternate filling: Use Soft Icing recipe (page 75).

A blanket of beautiful snow is covering every flaw and imperfection on the farm. Martha loves snow. She took the children outside and had a lively snowball battle with them. Then she taught them to make snow sculptures, and now a Papa Bear, Mama Bear, and Baby Bear stand along the front walk, guarding the yard.

They came trooping inside, all rosy-cheeked and merry. I told them they could help make peanut butter balls to dip in melted chocolate. Martha asked if she could make "saint hearts" (sand tarts). Soon the kitchen was filled with good smells.

(A Golden Sunbeam, 44-45)

Sand Tarts or Saint Hearts

1 c. shortening	1 t. salt
2 c. granulated sugar	2 t. baking powder
3 eggs	1 t. vanilla OR lemon extract
31/2 to 4 c. flour	

Cream shortening and sugar. Add eggs and flavoring; beat until fluffy. Add dry ingredients, and stir until medium-soft dough forms. Chill several hours in refrigerator. Roll very thin and cut in fancy shapes. Brush tops with rich milk and sprinkle with sugar and cinnamon. Decorate with pecan halves. Place 1 inch apart on greased cookie sheet, and bake at 350° for 8 to 10 minutes. Makes 4 to 5 dozen cookies.

Cherry Bonbons

1/2 c. soft butter	1 1/2 c. flour
3/4 c. powdered sugar	1/8 t. salt
1 t. vanilla	maraschino cherries

Mix all ingredients except cherries. If batter is dry, add one to two tablespoons cream. Make small balls with batter, putting a maraschino cherry inside each one and covering it completely. Place 1 to 2 inches apart on ungreased cookie sheet. Bake 10 to 12 minutes at 350°. When cookies are cool, dip tops in icing.

Icing:

1 c. powdered sugar	1 t. vanilla
2 T. cream	Few drops red food coloring (opt.)

December 22

I wonder, amid all this going to Christmas dinners, cooking, baking, candy making, and gift wrapping and exchanging: Do we stop often enough to ponder the real meaning of Christmas? Do we prepare our hearts to make room for Christ?

Tonight Martha was making candy, and the kitchen was filled with the good smells of melted chocolate, vanilla, cinnamon, dates, peanut butter, and coconut. Crist helped by cracking out all the English walnuts she needed, and Peter kept the woodbox filled with dry, split wood.

Dora made cherry bonbons and the traditional sand tarts sprinkled with red and green sugar. I did the cleaning up and dishwashing while they all traipsed outdoors to go sled riding in the moonlight. Nate and I walked out to watch them for a few minutes at bedtime. We were almost tempted to take a ride ourselves in the clear, cold air, with the moonlight shimmering on the ice-crusted snow.

(*A Golden Sunbeam*, 159-160)

Buckeyes

1 lb. peanut butter	1 package (12 oz.)
1 1/2 lb. powdered sugar	chocolate chips
1 c. butter OR margarine	1/2 stick paraffin

Mix peanut butter and sugar together like pie dough, then add butter or margarine. Roll mixture into balls and chill thoroughly. Melt chocolate chips and paraffin, and dip balls into this mixture to coat, leaving one spot uncovered to look like buckeyes.

Chocolate Drop Candies

3 c. sugar	2 egg whites, stiffly beaten
3/4 c. light corn syrup	1 t. vanilla
1/2 c. water	Coating chocolate

Combine sugar, corn syrup, and water in saucepan. Heat, stirring until dissolved. Boil to soft ball stage on candy thermometer— 245°. Pour hot syrup into beaten egg whites in thin stream, continuing to beat into very stiff peaks. Blend in vanilla and cool slightly. Shape into little balls of desired sizes and dip into melted coating chocolate.

Make other kinds of chocolate candies by dipping and coating clusters of raisins, peanuts, miniature marshmallows, coconut, crisped rice, chopped dates, or pretzels.

Store-Away Fudge

4 1/2 c. sugar
1/2 c. butter OR
  margarine
1 can sweetened
  condensed milk
2 large chocolate bars

2 c. chocolate chips
1 pint marshmallows
1 t. vanilla
1/2 t. black walnut flavoring (opt.)
1/2 c. chopped nuts (opt.)

Bring sugar, butter, and condensed milk to a boil, and boil for
7 minutes, or until the soft ball stage. Remove from heat and add
chocolate bars (cut into small pieces), chocolate chips,
marshmallows (cut into pieces), vanilla, and flavoring and nuts if
desired. Beat mixture until smooth and pour into buttered pan.

Desserts

9

Desserts

November 25

This afternoon we all went over to Ben Esh's to help get ready for the wedding. Isaac raked leaves, I helped clean the kitchen, and Anna helped cook the cornstarch pudding. That was fun! I really enjoyed being there. A wedding truly is a time of rejoicing.

There's a rosy sunset in the west tonight, and it looks for a sunny day tomorrow.

(*A Fruitful Vine*, 72)

Basic Vanilla Pudding

3/4 c. sugar	1/2 c. cold milk
1/3 c. cornstarch	3 1/2 c. milk, scalded
1/2 t. salt	1 t. vanilla
2 eggs, separated	1 T. butter

Combine dry ingredients, then stir in beaten egg yolks and cold milk. Beat mixture into hot milk, and stir over medium heat until it thickens. Add vanilla and butter. Fold in beaten egg whites, or top pudding with meringue.

Variation: For coconut pudding, add 1 cup of coconut. Top pudding with meringue and coconut.

Butterscotch Pudding

1 c. brown sugar	3 c. milk
2 eggs, beaten	2 T. butter OR margarine
3 T. flour	1 t. vanilla
1/4 t. salt	

Melt butter in skillet. Add sugar and salt and mix well. Slowly add 2 cups milk, and heat to boiling point. Make a paste by adding remaining milk to flour. Add to mixture, stirring constantly until thickened. Beat eggs. Add 1/2 cup hot mixture to eggs, then add eggs to pudding. Cook for 2 minutes and remove from heat. Add vanilla. Chill and garnish with ground peanuts, whipped cream, or sliced bananas.

November 20, Thanksgiving

Today was the wedding, Sally and Henry's. A wedding is a day of happiness and joy, feasting and celebration, and also a hallowed time, when two people step into holy matrimony together.

The spotlessly clean rooms were filled with chairs and benches. Tables in the cellar were loaded with prepared foods: cubed cheese, macaroni salad, dishes of pineapple tapioca, butterscotch pudding, chocolate cake, white cake, peaches, trays of cookies, jars of mixed candies.

(A Fruitful Vine, 37)

Wedding Tapioca

9 c. water	1 c. sugar
1/2 t. salt	1 (3-oz.) pkg. orange gelatin
1 1/2 c. tapioca	1 (3-oz.) pkg. lemon gelatin
(baby pearl)	2 (3-oz.) pkg. pineapple gelatin

Bring water and salt to boiling point. Add tapioca and boil until clear, stirring constantly. Remove from heat and stir in sugar and gelatin powders. Chill this mixture.

Variations: Add whipped cream, nuts, or fruit such as pineapple, bananas, or orange slices.

Chocolate Fudge Pudding

3 T. shortening
3/4 c. sugar
1 c. all-purpose flour
1/2 t. salt
1 1/2 t. baking powder
1/2 c. milk

1/2 c. nuts, chopped
1 c. brown sugar
1/4 c. cocoa
1/4 t. salt
1 1/4 c. boiling water

Cream shortening and white sugar. Mix flour, ½ teaspoon salt, and baking powder, and add alternately with milk to creamed mixture. Fold in nuts and pour batter into ungreased pan. Mix brown sugar, cocoa, and 1/4 teaspoon salt. Sprinkle mixture over top of batter but do not stir in. Pour boiling water over all, again not stirring it. Bake pudding at 350° for 40 to 45 minutes. Serve warm with whipped cream, ice cream, or milk.

Date Pudding

1 c. chopped dates
1 c. boiling water
1 c. sugar
1 1/2 c. all-purpose flour
1/2 c. chopped nuts

1 t. butter
1 t. vanilla
1 egg
2 t. soda
1/2 t. salt

Put dates into a bowl and pour boiling water over them. Let cool a little, then add other ingredients. Bake pudding at 325° for 30 to 40 minutes, then let cool. Chop up pudding before serving and mix whipped cream through it.

After the dishes were washed and Mary was resting in the bedroom, Nancy decided to make some cherry *Gnepplin* (dumplings).

First she got a can of sour cherries from the cellar and thickened them with clear jell. Then she mixed the flour, eggs, and milk. She stirred them until a smooth batter was formed, then dropped the batter, a teaspoon at a time, into boiling water.

Now let that boil for a few minutes, Nancy told herself. She went outside to sit on the porch glider to cool off.

"Yahoo, Nancy," called a voice from the road. Sally and Lakisha were in the spring wagon, pulled by the pony. "Come along for a ride," Sally called, motioning to Nancy.

Forgetting all about her *Gnepplin,* Nancy dashed out to the pony and hopped up on the seat beside the girls.

They went around what they called their square mile, then Sally reined the pony to a stop in front of Mary and Jacob's house.

Even before she reached the porch, Nancy smelled it. *Ach my, what's that awful odor?* she wondered. "Oh no, my *Gnepplin!*" she moaned.

She grabbed a potholder and ran outside with the burned black kettle. *What can I do with this awful mess?* she thought wildly.

Then she had a bright idea. She ran into the woodshed, grabbed a shovel, and furiously began to dig a hole in the garden. Quickly she scraped the dried and burned *Gnepplin* into the hole and began to cover them with dirt.

(*Summerville Days,* 54-57)

Cherry Dumplings

1 qt. canned sour cherries	2 c. flour
1 c. water	2 eggs
3 T. cornstarch	3/4 c. milk
Sugar to taste	2/3 t. salt

Bring cherries to boiling point. Combine cornstarch and water to make a paste. Add paste to cherries and cook until thickened, stirring constantly. Remove from heat, but keep warm. To make dumplings: Mix flour and salt, then make a well in the mixture and add eggs. Stir with a fork, and add milk to mixture. Stir until a smooth, thick batter is formed. Drop by teaspoonfuls into 1 1/2 quarts of boiling salt water. (Every fourth or fifth, time dip spoon in boiling water to keep batter from sticking to spoon.) Boil one minute more after all batter is in the kettle. Remove from heat and drain through colander. Melt and brown 1/4 cup butter and pour over dumplings. To serve, pour thickened cherries on top.

Cherry Cream Cheese Delight

Crust:
2 c. crushed graham crackers
1 stick melted butter

Mix and press into bottom of 9"-x-13" pan.

Filling:
8-oz. pkg. cream cheese
1 1/2 c. powdered sugar
2 pkgs. whipped topping mix (mixed as directed on pkg.)

Mix together and pour over graham cracker crust.

Topping:
1 qt. sour cherries, thickened as for pie OR
    1 can cherry pie filling

Spread on top of cream cheese filling, and refrigerate pie for several hours before serving.

As we drove in the lane, I spied three little faces at the window. Dora was waving to us. It was a warm, cheery welcome, the babies crowding around me happily, and a wonderful aroma coming from the kitchen.

Already I'm wondering how we managed without Priscilla. She had a fire·crackling in the grate, a kettle of mush bubbling merrily on the stove, and apple crisp baking in the oven. Dora ran to me, threw her arms around me, and cried, "Mama!"

I don't know who was gladder to see me, she or the babies. They both wiggled all over with delight and held out their arms to be picked up.

Thank you, God, for my precious family. May I never take any of them for granted.

(*A Winding Path*, 20)

Apple Crisp

3 c. sliced or chopped apples	1 T. water
1 T. flour	1/2 c. rolled oats
1/4 c. sugar	1/4 t. salt
1 t. cinnamon	1/4 c. butter OR margarine
1/8 t. salt	1/3 c. brown sugar

Mix apples, flour, white sugar, cinnamon, and 1/8 teaspoon salt, and put in greased casserole. Blend oats, 1/4 teaspoon salt, butter, and brown sugar with pastry blender, and sprinkle on top. Bake at 375° for 35 minutes.

Winter still has us in its icy grip. The children happily go skating or sledding every evening after school. Then they come in whining that they are cold and half starved. A least that is something that is easily remedied. Are we thankful enough that we have warm houses and plenty to eat?

A row of pretty icicles hang from around the barn eaves and from the porch roof. Peter brought one in tonight that was all of three feet long and clear as crystal. I told him to gather more of them. We put them into a burlap sack, smashed them up with the back of the ax, and used them to make homemade vanilla ice cream.

It's too bad that there aren't icicles in summertime to make ice cream with. In the winter we have to huddle around the stove to get warm after eating it.

Rudy stopped in to chat a few minutes tonight, and to warm himself by the fire. Instead we chilled him, by giving him a bowl of ice cream.

(*A Golden Sunbeam*, 115)

Vanilla Ice Cream

1 qt. milk	2 T. milk
2 c. sugar	1 pkg. unflavored gelatin
1/2 c. cornstarch	3 t. cold milk
1/4 t. salt	1 qt. thick cream
1 c. cold milk	1 t. vanilla
4 egg yolks	4 egg whites, well-beaten

Scald quart of milk, then add sugar, cornstarch, and salt, which have been blended into the 1 cup of cold milk. Cook mixture until thick. Add egg yolks, mixed with 2 tablespoons of milk, then cook for 1 minute. Add gelatin, which has been soaked in the 3 teaspoons of cold milk. Remove cooked custard from stove, and let cool. Add cream, vanilla, and well-beaten egg whites, then freeze. Makes 1 gallon.

Variations: For chocolate ice cream, mix ½ cup cocoa with a little boiling water, and add to above recipe before freezing. For raspberry ice cream, add crushed raspberries instead of cocoa and water.

February 14

Valentine's Day. At school they had a Valentine's Day party of sorts. Each scholar took an ingredient for home-made raspberry ice cream—eggs, milk, sugar, cream, vanilla, instant clear gelatin, a jar of canned raspberries, and salt for freezing it. In the afternoon the girls mixed the ingredients in Eli's big twelve-quart, hand-cranked ice cream freezer, while the boys went to the pond with an ax and a sack for the ice.

They all took turns cranking, and when it was done, they had an ice cream party. Teacher Melvin treated them with heart-shaped cookies that Barbianne had made. After the treats were eaten, they passed out the homemade valentines.

(*A Golden Sunbeam*, 116)

Hot Fudge Sauce

1 1/2 c. evaporated milk   1/2 t. salt
2 c. sugar   1/4 c. butter OR margarine
4 squares unsweetened chocolate   1 t. vanilla
   (4 oz. or less) OR cocoa

Heat milk and sugar to rolling boil, stirring constantly. Boil for
1 minute. Add chocolate and salt, stirring until chocolate is melted.
Beat with rotary beater until smooth. Remove from heat and stir in
butter and vanilla. Serve hot on ice cream, or chill if desired.
Makes 3 cups.

Strawberry or Raspberry Topping

1 qt. mashed strawberries   1 pkg. pectin
  OR raspberries   crystals
1 qt. sugar   1 c. boiling water

Mix strawberries and sugar until sugar is dissolved. Dissolve
pectin crystals in boiling water, bring to a boil, and immediately
stir into berry mixture. Stir for 5 minutes, then refrigerate, or put
into jars and freeze.

Beverages

10

Beverages

Mmmm! Nancy wondered what smelled so good when she opened the kitchen door. Was it fresh brewed meadow tea and bacon and eggs?

Several boards had been put into the table to make it longer. A clean white tablecloth was spread over it, and it was set with Mary's pretty Sunday dishes with purple violets around the rim.

Dad had seated himself at the head of the table, and Jacob handed him the family Bible. He began to read the Beatitudes.

Nancy's soul felt bathed in peace and contentment as she listened to Dad's voice reading. *There's no place I'd rather be than with my family,* she thought. Although Joe and Omar were missing, she knew she would soon see them again. For now, this was enough.

"Let's bow our heads for prayer," Dad said.

During the silent prayer, Nancy listened to the ticking of the clock. She peeked at the food in front of her: a platter of steaming eggs and bacon, fried cornmeal mush, a bowl of hot cooked oatmeal, pitchers of creamy milk, and a cup of hot meadow tea at each plate. Guiltily Nancy squeezed her eyes shut.

"For health and strength and daily food, we praise thy name, O Lord," she whispered.

(*Summerville Days,* 133-134)

Pamela came this afternoon, asking if she could buy some spinach for a salad she's making. Of course, I gave her all she wanted and told her to come back for more whenever she wants. She has carried quite a few messages for us and done other favors, and we have lots to spare, anyhow.

She stayed to chat awhile, as she usually does. I gave her a cup of freshly brewed meadow tea, and she said she'll never drink Lipton tea again.

(*A Treasured Friendship*, 138)

Meadow Tea

(Use homegrown garden teas—spearmint, balsam or applemint, or peppermint— either freshly picked, or dried for winter use.)

    1 handful fresh mint leaves OR
     4 t. dried mint leaves
    4 c. boiling water

Bring fresh water to a bubbling boil. Pour small amount of boiling water in ceramic or glass container, allow to sit for several minutes to heat container, then pour out. Put tea leaves in container and pour boiling water over them, allowing to steep for 3 to 5 minutes. (If leaves remain in tea too long, it will be bitter.) Serve hot or cold with sugar and lemon or cream, as desired. When sweetening iced tea, use about 1/4 cup sugar to each quart of tea.

Iced Tea Syrup

11/2 to 2 c. sugar
4 c. water
2 c. garden tea, tightly packed
(use leaves and small stem ends)

Combine sugar and water in stainless steel saucepan or granite pan. Boil for several minutes. Remove from heat and add garden tea. Make sure all leaves are covered with water. Cover pan and let steep for approximately 6 hours. Strain and refrigerate.

To serve, mix one part syrup with 3 parts (or more, if desired) ice and water. Syrup can be used immediately, or poured into ice cube trays and frozen for later use. This recipe makes 4 cups of concentrate, or 3 quarts of tea.

Peppermint Water

Sweeten a pitcher of cold water. Dip a toothpick into a bottle of peppermint oil, then swish it in the water. Do this a few times until mint taste is as strong as desired. Stir water before tasting. (Synthetic peppermint oil is not recommended.) This is a good drink for people working under the sun on hot days.

Summer Sparkle Punch

2 pkg. (3 oz.) strawberry gelatin
2 c. boiling water
2 (12 oz.) cans frozen lemonade
3 (28 oz.) bottles ginger ale

Partially thaw frozen lemonade. Dissolve gelatin powder in boiling water, stir in lemonade, and add ginger ale. Makes 1 gallon.

Lemonade

6 lemons   21/2 qt. water
11/2 c. sugar

Slice lemons in thin rings and place in pitcher or bowl. To extract juice, add sugar and pound and crush with wooden mallet or spoon. Let stand 20 minutes, then add cold water and ice cubes. Stir until well blended. Makes 3 quarts.

October 15

We've been hearing a cricket all fall, from somewhere underneath the sideboard. Peter has tried to capture it, but I hope he doesn't succeed. I like to hear his friendly chirping.

Our south field is dotted with corn shocks this year, and the wild geese are winging their way south. The apple trees are loaded with fruit, so we'll have plenty of cider.

(A Golden Sunbeam, 104)

Icy Spiced Cider

6 c. sweet cider   1/2 t. grated lemon rind
20 whole cloves   1/2 t. grated orange rind
3 sticks cinnamon

Combine spices and 3 cups cider and place over low heat. Bring to boiling point and simmer 5 minutes. Remove from heat and let stand 30 minutes. Add remaining cider, orange rind, and lemon rind. Chill. When ready to serve, pour over ice cubes. Garnish with orange or lemon slices. Makes 8-10 servings.

Hot Spiced Cider

1 qt. apple cider
1/2 of 3-inch cinnamon
  stick, crushed
1/3 t. allspice

1/2 t. whole cloves
1/8 t. salt
1/3 c. brown sugar

Combine cider, spices, and salt in saucepan, crumbling the cinnamon. Simmer 10 minutes. Add brown sugar and strain. Serve hot. Makes 5 servings.

December 20

We're sure having our share of snow! During the night another winter snowstorm howled down from the north country and covered our valley with beautiful drifts of new-fallen snow.

In the afternoon the wind stopped, and the sun came out. We bundled up and went for a tramp through the snow, following the creek and looking for the tracks of wild animals. Our snowshoes made tracks of their own.

We saw bunny tracks, lacy-looking bird tracks (or maybe it was mice), and even fox tracks. The drifted snow was pure white and breathtakingly beautiful.

Nate had supper ready when we came in, rosy-cheeked and famished. Tramping through the snow certainly whets one's appetite. Mush and eggs with sand tarts and hot chocolate sure tasted good even though it wasn't breakfast. I'm so glad he learned how to cook while he was still a bachelor. What a dear husband and father he is now!

(*A Golden Sunbeam*, 111-112)

Hot Chocolate

2 squares unsweetened chocolate (2 oz.)
1/3 c. sugar
1/8 t. salt
1/2 c. boiling water
1 qt. milk

Grate chocolate in top of double boiler, or melt in microwave. Add sugar, salt, and boiling water, and stir to make a smooth paste. Place pan over direct heat and cook syrup 3 minutes. Add milk gradually and heat to boiling point. Beat until frothy. Add whipped cream or a marshmallow to each cup. Makes 6 servings. *Note*: If using ready-made chocolate syrup, add 2 tablespoons for each cup of milk.

Hot Cocoa

3 T. cocoa powder   1/8 t. salt
1/3 c. sugar   6 marshmallows
1/2 c. warm water   1/2 t. vanilla (opt.)
1 qt. milk

Mix sugar, salt, and cocoa together. Add warm water and stir to a smooth paste. Cook for 3 minutes. Heat milk and add slowly to cocoa mixture. Stir until well blended. Add vanilla. Put a marshmallow in each cup. Pour cocoa over marshmallows.

Hot Chocolate Mix

8 c. dry milk powder
2 c. sugar
1 (16-oz.) can hot chocolate mix
1/2 t. salt
1 (8-oz.) jar coffee creamer

Mix ingredients well. Store in cool, dry place. To serve, fill cup 1/3 of the way with mix, then fill with boiling water. Stir. Makes approximately 14 cups of mix, or 42 cups of hot chocolate.

Snacks and Spreads

11

Snacks and Spreads

January 26

Brrr! It's cold! Fifteen degrees below zero this morning! It feels cozy sitting by the stove, feet in the bake oven, with a dish of freshly exploded popcorn and a bowl of juicy red apples beside me. The sun shone brightly this afternoon and warmed things up considerably, and the children begged to go skating.

The children had great fun, slipping, sliding, and falling down, laughing and getting up again, then soon flopping down again. As I sat on the bank watching them, I was thinking that learning to skate is a bit like learning to walk in the Spirit and living the Christian life. So often we fall and have to pick ourselves up, ask for forgiveness, and start over again.

(A Joyous Heart, 131)

Golden Popcorn

1 c. sugar	1 t. vinegar
1/2 c. baking molasses (dark)	1/4 t. soda
1/2 c. corn syrup	5 qt. popped corn
1 T. butter	1 c. peanuts
2 T. water	

Mix sugar, molasses, syrup, butter, water, and vinegar. Cook mixture until it forms a hard ball (265°) when dropped into cold water. Stir frequently during last part of cooking to prevent scorching. Remove from heat and add soda, then stir lightly. While still foaming, pour over popcorn and peanuts and mix together. Pour mixture into buttered, flat pan. When cool, crumble into small pieces.

Peanut Butter Popcorn Balls

3 or 4 qt. popped corn	1/2 c. chunky peanut butter
1/2 c. sugar	1/2 t. vanilla
1/2 c. light corn syrup	1/8 t. salt

Combine sugar and corn syrup in saucepan, and heat to a rolling boil, stirring constantly. Remove from heat. Stir in peanut butter, vanilla, and salt, until well blended. Pour over corn, stirring until well coated. Shape into balls, if desired.

Soft Pretzels

1 pkg. dry yeast	4 to 5 c. all-purpose flour
1 1/4 c. warm water	Butter as needed
1 t. sugar	4 t. soda
2 t. salt	Coarse salt for sprinkling

Dissolve yeast in 1/4 cup warm water. Stir in additional cup of warm water, and the sugar. Pour yeast mixture into bowl, and add salt. Beat in flour to make a stiff dough. Knead for 10 minutes, or until dough is elastic. Place in bowl and spread with butter. Cover and let rise for 45 minutes or until double in size. Shape dough into sticks or twists, half the thickness of desired finished pretzel.

Bring 4 cups of water to boiling; add soda. Drop in pretzels, 3 at a time. Boil for 1 minute or until pretzels float. Remove, drain, and place on buttered cookie sheets. Sprinkle with coarse salt. Bake at 475° for 12 minutes or until golden brown. To make pretzels crisp, lay them on cookie sheet and heat in warm oven (200°) for 2 hours.

It feels so good to sit down and rest my weary feet tonight. We had a busy day of getting ready for church here tomorrow, and now I think I can say we're actually ready. The house is spick-and-span, the folding doors are opened, and the benches are all set in place.

Rudy and Barbianne were here to help, also Grandpa Daves and the families of neighbors Eli and Emanuel. The *Schnitzboi* (dried-apple pies) are all made and waiting on the pantry shelves. The church spread (a combination of peanut butter and molasses) is mixed, and the washhouse table is filled with loaves of freshly baked brown bread.

Crocks of smearcase (cottage cheese) are ready. Cans of red beets and pickles are on the shelf, and the dried meadow tea from last summer is waiting to be brewed. As usual, it will be a quick and simple meal.

(*A Golden Sunbeam*, 82)

Church Spread

1 gal. pancake syrup
1 gal. marshmallow creme
4 c. peanut butter

Mix ingredients thoroughly.

Caramel Spread

2 c. brown sugar
2 c. granulated sugar
1 c. corn syrup

1 c. water
2 egg whites

Cook ingredients, bringing mixture to full boil. Let cool.

Pineapple Cheese Spread

8 oz. cottage cheese
2 t. sugar
1/2 c. well-drained, crushed pineapple
1/4 t. vanilla

Process in blender until smooth. Makes 11/4 cups.

Ham Spread

3 T. mayonnaise OR salad dressing
1 c. ground cooked ham
1/2 t. prepared mustard
1/2 c. shredded Swiss cheese

Combine mayonnaise and mustard, then mix in ham and cheese.

November 14

Matthew's affectionate, loving baby ways have been a balm to my troubled soul. He's been trying to say "Miriam," and it comes out sounding more like "Mammy." That thrills my heart! It even drew a chuckle out of Isaac when he heard it.

Today I sat at the sewing machine, making little shirts for Matthew and an apron for myself. The mornings are cool and frosty. I've been cleaning out the garden, carrying in pumpkins, and digging carrots. On the stove I have a drying pan of apples, which makes the whole kitchen smell good. Isaac loves dried apples, and even Matthew likes to chew on them.

(*A Fruitful Vine*, 35)

Apple Schnitz (Dried Apples)

Put peeled, cut-up apples in the sun with a screened cover. Or dry in the oven at very low heat for 4 to 6 hours. Old window screens make perfect oven racks, and let apples dry on both sides at once.

(Miriam notes: "Most of the plain people have special drying pans. These are big, rectangular, steel pans with a hole in one corner to pour water into a lower compartment. The apples dry on top. These pans can also be used on a gas or electric stove.")

Pickles and Preserves

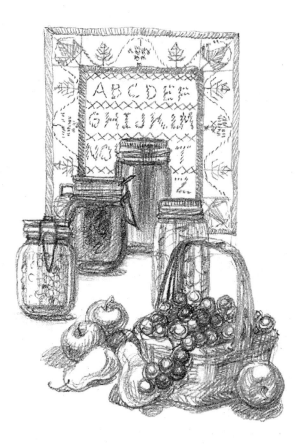

12

Pickles and Preserves

After church services were over, Sally, Barbie, and Nancy went outside for a breath of fresh air. The men were setting up tables and benches in the kitchen and *Sitzschtupp* (sitting room). The women were busy getting food ready for the table.

They put on plates of homemade bread and rolls, red beets, pickles, cup cheese, dishes of church spread (a mixture of peanut butter and molasses), *Schnitzboi* (dried-apple pie), and cups of steaming hot coffee and tea.
(*Summerville Days*, 142-143)

Dollar Bread and Butter Pickles

4 qt. sliced cucumbers (40 to 50)	1 T. turmeric (optional)
1/2 c. salt	1 qt. vinegar
2 qt. sliced onions	1 T. ginger
4 c. sugar	1 T. celery seed
2 T. mustard	

Gently stir salt into thinly sliced cucumbers. Cover with ice cubes and let stand for 2 or 3 hours, until cucumbers are crisp and cold. Add more ice if most of it melts. Drain cucumbers and add onions. Combine remaining ingredients and bring mixture quickly to a boil, boiling for 10 minutes. Add cucumber and onion slices and bring to boiling point. Pack at once in hot jars. Process in a boiling water bath for 30 minutes. Remove jars from canner and complete sealing. Makes 8 pints.

Overnight Dill Pickles

20 to 25 dill-sized (4-inch)
  cucumbers
Powdered alum
Fresh dill, with seed
Small hot red peppers

4 c. vinegar
1 c. pickling salt
3 qt. water
Washed grape leaves (opt.)

Wash cucumbers. Put into pan of cold water and let stand overnight. Next morning, pack cucumbers in hot, sterile quart jars. Into each jar measure 1/8 teaspoon alum. Add 2 heads of dill and 1 small hot red pepper. Combine vinegar, salt, and water and heat to boiling. Fill jars with hot liquid. Process and seal, and allow to stand for 6 weeks. Add a washed grape leaf or two on the top for green coloring.

Pickled Red Beets

3 qt. small beets
3 c. vinegar
2 T. salt

4 c. sugar
1 1/2 c. water
2 cinnamon sticks (opt.)

Cook beets. Combine rest of ingredients and boil to a syrup. Pour boiling syrup over beets in hot jars, then seal. Process in boiling water bath for 10 to 15 minutes.

August 17

A long day. We canned over fifty quarts of chowchow. We have a satisfying feeling as we look over the rows of jars of colorful vegetables—lima beans, corn, peppers, pickles, carrots, and string beans. It's a lot of work, but it's worth it. Now, next winter when the snow is flying outside, we can go to the cellar for a jar of delicious chowchow.

(A Joyous Heart, 63)

Chowchow

1 qt. cucumbers, diced
1 qt. string beans
1 qt. lima beans
1 qt. corn
1 pt. celery
1 pt. green peppers

1 pt. red peppers
1 c. small onions
1 T. dry mustard
2 c. sugar
1 qt. vinegar

Chop vegetables to desired size and cook separately. Cook until tender, but not soft. Drain vegetables and mix together. Combine sugar, mustard, and vinegar and bring to a boil. Add mixed vegetables to hot liquid and bring to boiling point. Pack into hot jars, process in boiling water bath, and seal.

Corn Relish

12 ears corn
1 head cabbage
6 peppers
2 stalks celery
1 t. celery seed

1 t. mustard seed
1 c. sugar
1/4 c. salt
1 pt. vinegar

Cut corn from cobs. Chop cabbage, peppers (remove seeds), and celery in food chopper, using coarse blade. Mix with rest of ingredients and boil mixture for 30 minutes. Pack in hot jars, process, and seal.

Apple butter cooking time! We don't make as much as some people do, but it's a day-long job. *Schnitzing, schnitzing,* and more *schnitzing* (cutting) of apples. Then filling the big copper furnace kettle with the chopped apples and having someone constantly stirring them with the big wooden stirrer. No wonder the Dutch word for apple butter is *Lattwarick,* which means "a lot of work."

Yet just the aroma of the cooking apples is worth it. Neighbors "Drafty" Dave and Annie came to help, and we'll share the finished product with them.

(*A Winding Path,* 20-21)

Copper Kettle Apple Butter

20 gal. fresh apple cider
8 gal. apples, peeled, cored, and chopped
15 lb. sugar
1 T. oil of cinnamon (opt.)

Use a large (30- to 40-gallon) copper kettle. Heat cider to boiling, and let cook until reduced to about half former amount. Add half the apples and cook until soft. Add remaining apples and cook until soft, stirring frequently. Add sugar and stir constantly to prevent burning. When a little of the cooled butter is of good spreading consistency, remove butter from fire. Add oil of cinnamon, if desired, and mix thoroughly. Makes approximately 12 gallons.

Apple Butter (*Stove Method*)

2 qt. apple cider
4 qt. apples, peeled
and sliced
2 c. sugar

2 c. dark corn syrup
1 t. powdered cinnamon
OR ¼ t. oil of cinnamon

Boil cider in heavy kettle until reduced to 1 quart. Peel apples, core, and slice in thin pieces. Add apples to cider and cook slowly until mixture begins to thicken. Stir frequently. Add sugar, syrup, and cinnamon. Continue to cook until a little of the butter, when cooled on a plate, is of good spreading consistency. Makes 5 to 6 pints.

October 15

We had a pear *schnitzing* (frolic) to make pear butter. It was a warm evening, so we sat outside under the grape arbor, with only a lantern and the warm glow of the harvest moon for lighting. Grandpa Daves, Rudy and Barbianne, and even Pam came to help.

Everyone seemed to be in a jovial mood. The silos are filled, and cellars are filled with canned goods, and barns and granaries are well stocked for another year. Harvesting is nearly done, and God has again blessed us with plenty to eat and seen us through another season.

(*A Golden Sunbeam*, 105)

Pear Butter

1/2 gal. pears
4 c. sugar

1 qt. light corn syrup
Nutmeg OR cinnamon (opt.)

Cook pears in small amount of water, then mash as you would apples for applesauce. Add sugar, corn syrup, and spice (if desired). Bake mixture in 350° oven or simmer on top of stove until it is spreading consistency. *Note:* When cooking on top of the stove, take care to avoid scorching.

Grape Butter

1 qt. whole grapes
4 c. sugar
2 T. water

Cook ingredients for 20 minutes, then put through fruit press or colander. Pour into jars, process, and seal.

July 11

One by one, the shelves in the cellar are filling up. First it was rhubarb, then strawberries, peas, cherries, string beans, pickles, and soon we'll be canning applesauce from the early apples.

Dora and Sadie are good helpers. Even little Crist willingly trots up and down the steps, bringing up empty jars as we need them, and carrying cooled cans of applesauce down to the cellar, one at a time, carefully!

Yesterday Dora announced that we already have over a thousand quarts of canned goods. We will also freeze some things. Frozen food tastes better than the canned, and it's less work to put up the food. But we use the locker in town, and that's not as handy as a freezer at home.

(*A Treasured Friendship*, 23-24)

Applesauce

Wash apples thoroughly. Cut into halves or quarters, removing stems, and bruised or defective spots. Put apples in a large kettle, and cook in water (3 cups or less for 3 to 4 gallons of apples) until soft and mushy, about 15 to 20 minutes. (Stir occasionally, especially when beginning to cook, to prevent sticking.) Remove apples from heat and immediately put through a sieve or strainer. If sauce is too thick, add water, but not too much, since adding sugar will also thin it. Sugar may be added in the bowl or to each container as you fill it. To freeze, allow applesauce to cool completely. Fill and seal plastic freezer containers, leaving 1 inch headspace. To can, use a funnel to fill jars, leaving 1 inch headspace. Stir with a wooden spoon to remove air bubbles. Tighten lids and process for 25 minutes in a boiling water bath.

Recipe Sources

All recipes, unless otherwise noted, are reprinted from *Amish Cooking,* copyright © 1980 by Pathway Publishing Corporation; published by Herald Press, Scottdale, Pennsylvania 15683; and used by permission. The other recipes are also used by permission of Herald Press, as listed here:

From Carrie Bender's personal collection: Miriam's Favorite Granola, 13; Miriam's Grapenuts, 13; Miriam's Apple Bake, 16; Succotash (Miriam's Recipe), 44; Hay Stack, 36; Sadie's Salad Dressing, 56; Miriam's Black Raspberry Cream Pie, 63; Miriam's Church Cookies, 81; Cherry Bonbons, 86; Cherry Cream Cheese Delight, 95; Miriam's Church Spread, 113.

From Mary Clemens Meyer's personal collection: Oatmeal with Raisins, 12; Blueberry Pie, 60; Applesauce, 125.

From *Mennonite Community Cookbook,* by Mary Emma Showalter, copyright © 1978 by Mary Emma Showalter, published by Herald Press: Waffles, 14; Roast Chicken, 37; New Peas and Potatoes, 42; Scalloped Corn 43; Creamed Limas, 44; Scalloped Potatoes, 46; Potato Puffs, 46; Dried Schnitz (Snitz) Pie, 63; Pumpkin Pie, 64; Sand Tarts or Saint Hearts, 85; Butterscotch Pudding, 92; Cherry Dumplings (Knepplies), 95; Meadow Tea (Tea), 104 (adapted); Lemonade, 106; Icy Spiced Cider (Spiced Cider), 106; Hot Chocolate, 108; Hot Cocoa, 108; Chowchow, 121; Copper Kettle Apple Butter (Apple Butter–Large Amount), 122; Apple Butter, Stove Method (Apple Butter–Small Amount), 123.

From *Mennonite Country-Style Recipes and Kitchen Secrets,* by Esther H. Shank, copyright © 1987 by Herald Press: Creamed Onions, 42; Oatmeal Raisin Cookies (Old-Fashioned Oatmeal Cookies), 83; Whoopie Pies, 84; Chocolate Drop Candies, 87; Iced Tea Syrup, 105; Hot Spiced Cider (Spicy Cider), 107; Hot Chocolate Mix, 108; Peanut Butter Popcorn Balls, 112; Pineapple Cheese Spread, 114; Ham Spread, 114.

From *More-with-Less Cookbook,* by Doris Janzen Longacre, copyright © 1976 by Herald Press: Oven Egg Casserole (Old-Fashioned Bread Omelet), 12; Apple Schnitz (Dried Apples), 115.

From *Wonderful Good Cooking from Amish Country Kitchens,* copyright © 1974 by Amish Country Publishers of Holmes County, Berlin, Ohio 44610; published by Herald Press: Apple Pancakes, 15; White Bread, 19; Spiced Cabbage, 42.

Index of Recipes

The Author

The author's pen name is Carrie Bender. She is a member of an old order group. With her husband and children, she lives among the Amish in Lancaster County, Pennsylvania. Her books thus far are listed on page 2.

Her Miriam's Journal Series is well appreciated by a wide reading public. These stories in journal form are about a middle-aged Amish woman who for the first time finds love leading to marriage. Miriam and Nate raise an active family and face life with faith and faithfulness. Bender portrays their ups and downs through the seasons, year after year.

Bender is also the popular author of the Whispering Brook Series, books about fun-loving Nancy Petersheim, as she grows up surrounded by her close-knit Amish family, her friends, and her church community. This series is for children and a general audience.

Library Journal says, "Bender's writing is sheer poetry. It leads readers to ponder the intimate relationship of people and nature."

回

The Compiler and Editor

Mary Clemens Meyer grew up in Lansdale, Pennsylvania, the daughter of a Mennonite pastor. Her lively household included six siblings and a live-in grandmother.

Meyer graduated from Christopher Dock Mennonite High School and has a degree in art and communication from Goshen (Indiana) College. She has written Herald Press curriculum for Bible school and Sunday school, including two quarters of the Jubilee early-childhood materials.

Walking with Jesus is a Herald Press book of peacemaking stories which she wrote for children. She is also the editor of *On the Line*, a Herald Press magazine for children aged 9 to 14 years.

Meyer developed the idea for *Miriam's Cookbook* and compiled it with the cooperation of Carrie Bender. She used material from Bender's books and recipe files, along with other Herald Press resources and her own recipes.

Mary and her husband, Ron, are members of the Kingview Mennonite Church of Scottdale, Pennsylvania. They have three children.